WORD TRANSLATIONS

GRE Math Strategy Guide

The Word Translations guide educates students in the art of translating challenging word problems into organized data, as well as providing structured frameworks for attacking each question type.

Word Translations GRE Strategy Guide, First Edition

10-digit International Standard Book Number: 1-935707-06-X
13-digit International Standard Book Number: 978-1-935707-06-6

Note: *GRE, Graduate Record Examination, Educational Testing Services,* and *ETS*
are all registered trademarks of Educational Testing Services, which neither
sponsors nor is affiliated in any way with this product.

8 GUIDE INSTRUCTIONAL SERIES

Math GRE Strategy Guides

Algebra
(ISBN: 978-1-935707-02-8)

Fractions, Decimals, & Percents
(ISBN: 978-1-935707-03-5)

Geomctry
(ISBN: 978-1-935707-04-2)

Number Properties
(ISBN: 978 1 035707-05-9)

Word Translations
(ISBN: 978-1-935707-06-6)

Quantitative Comparisons & Data Interpretation
(ISBN. 978-1-935707-07-3)

Verbal GRE Strategy Guides

Reading Comprehension & Essays
(ISBN: 978-1-935707-08-0)

ASA: Antonyms, Sentence Completion, Analogies
(ISBN: 978-1-935707-09-7)

Manhattan GRE

September 1st, 2010

Dear Student,

Thank you for picking up one of the Manhattan GRE Strategy Guides—we hope that it refreshes your memory of junior-high school math that you haven't used in years. Maybe it will even teach you a new thing or two.

As with most accomplishments, there were many people involved in the book that you're holding. First and foremost is Zeke Vanderhoek, the founder of MG Prep. Zeke was a lone tutor in New York when he started the Company in 2000. Now, ten years later, the Company has Instructors and offices nationwide and contributes to the studies and successes of thousands of students each year.

Our Manhattan GRE Strategy Guides are based on the continuing experiences of our Instructors and our students. On the Company side, we are indebted to many of our Instructors, including but not limited to Jen Dziura, Stacey Koprince, David Mahler, Chris Ryan, Michael Schwartz, and Tommy Wallach, all of whom either wrote or edited the books to their present form. Dan McNaney and Cathy Huang provided their formatting expertise to make the books as user-friendly as possible. Last, many people, too numerous to list here but no less appreciated, assisted in the development of the online resources that accompany this guide.

At Manhattan GRE, we continually aspire to provide the best Instructors and resources possible. We hope that you'll find our dedication manifest in this book. If you have any comments or questions, please e-mail me at andrew.yang@manhattangre.com. I'll be sure that your comments reach Chris and the rest of the team—and I'll read them too.

Best of luck in preparing for the GRE!

Sincerely,

Andrew Yang
President
Manhattan GRE

HOW TO ACCESS YOUR ONLINE STUDY CENTER

If you...

 are a registered Manhattan GRE student

and have received this book as part of your course materials, you have AUTOMATIC access to ALL of our online resources. To access these resources, follow the instructions in the Welcome Guide provided to you at the start of your program. Do NOT follow the instructions below.

 **purchased this book from the Manhattan GRE Online store or at one of our Centers**

1. Go to: http://www.manhattangre.com/studycenter.cfm

2. Log in using the username and password used when your account was set up.

 purchased this book at a retail location

1. Go to: http://www.manhattangre.com/access.cfm

2. Log in or create an account.

3. Follow the instructions on the screen.

Your one year of online access begins on the day that you register your book at the above URL.

You only need to register your product ONCE at the above URL. To use your online resources any time AFTER you have completed the registration process, login to the following URL: http://www.manhattangre.com/studycenter.cfm

Please note that online access is non-transferable. This means that only NEW and UNREGISTERED copies of the book will grant you online access. Previously used books will not provide any online resources.

 purchased an e-book version of this book

Email a copy of your purchase receipt to books@manhattangre.com to activate your resources.

For any technical issues, email books@manhattangre.com or call 800-576-4628.

Introduction, and How to Use Manhattan GRE's Strategy Guides

We know that you're looking to succeed on the GRE so that you can go to graduate school and do the things you want to do in life.

We also know that you might not have done math since high school, and that you may never have learned words like "adumbrate" or "sangfroid." We know that it's going to take hard work on your part to get a top GRE score, and that's why we've put together the only set of books that will take you from the basics all the way up to the material you need to master for a near-perfect score, or whatever your score goal may be.

How a Computer Adaptive Test Works

On paper-based tests, top scores are achieved by solving a mix of easy and medium questions, with a few hard ones at the end. The GRE is totally different.

The GRE is a computer adaptive test (or "CAT"). That means that the better you do, the harder the material you will see (and the worse you do, the easier the material you will see). Your ultimate score isn't based on how many questions you got right—it's based on "testing into" a high level of difficulty, and then performing well enough to stay at that difficulty level. In other words, you *want* to see mostly hard questions.

This book was written by a team of test prep professionals, including instructors who have scored perfect 1600s repeatedly on the GRE, and who have taught and tutored literally thousands of students at all levels of performance. We don't just focus on "tricks"—on a test that adapts to your performance, it's important to know the real material being tested.

Speed and Pacing

Most people can sum up the numbers from 1–20, if they have enough time. Most people can also tell you whether 789×791 is bigger than 788×792, if they have enough time. Few people can do these things in the 1–2 minutes per problem allotted on the GRE.

If you've taken a practice test (visit www.manhattangre.com for information about this), you may have had serious trouble finishing the test before time ran out. On the GRE, it is extremely important that you finish every question. (You also may not skip questions or return to any previously answered question). In these books, you'll find ways to do things fast—very fast.

As a reference, here's about how much time you should spend on each problem type on the GRE:

Analogies – **45 seconds**

Antonyms – **30 seconds**

Sentence Correction – **1 minute**

Reading Comprehension – **1.5 minutes**

Problem Solving and Data Interpretation – **2 minutes**

Quantitative Comparison – **1 min 15 seconds**

Of course, no one can time each question this precisely while taking the actual test—instead, you will see a timer on the screen that counts down (from 30 minutes on Verbal, and from 45 minutes on Quant), and you must keep an eye on that clock and manage time as you go. Manhattan GRE's strategies will help you solve questions extremely efficiently.

How to Use These Materials

Manhattan GRE's materials are comprehensive. But keep in mind that, depending on your score goal, it may not be necessary to "get" absolutely everything. Grad schools only see your overall Quantitative, Verbal, and Writing scores—they don't see exactly which strengths and weaknesses went into creating those scores.

You may be enrolled in one of our courses, in which case you already have a syllabus telling you in what order you should approach the books. But if you bought this book online or at a bookstore, feel free to approach the books—and even the chapters within the books—in whatever order works best for you. *For the most part, the books, and the chapters within them, are independent; you don't have to master one section before moving on to the next.* So if you're having a hard time with something in particular, you can make a note to come back to it later and move on to another section. Similarly, it may not be necessary to solve every single practice problem for every section. As you go through the material, continually assess whether you understand and can apply the principles in each individual section and chapter. The best way to do this is to solve the Check Your Skills and Practice Problems throughout. If you're confident you have a concept or method down, feel free to move on. If you struggle with something, make note of it for further review. Stay active in your learning and oriented toward the test—it's easy to read something and think you understand it, only to have trouble applying it in the 1–2 minutes you have to solve a problem.

Study Skills

As you're studying for the GRE, try to integrate your learning into your everyday life. For example, vocabulary is a big part of the GRE, as well as something you just can't "cram" for—you're going to want to do at least a little bit of vocab every day. So, try to learn and internalize a little bit at a time, switching up topics often to help keep things interesting.

Keep in mind that, while many of your study materials are on paper (including ETS's most recent source of official GRE questions, *Practicing to Take the GRE General Test 10th Edition*), your exam will be administered on a computer. The testing center will provide you with pencils and a booklet of bound, light-blue paper. If you run out, you may request a new booklet, but you may only have one at a time. Because this is a computer-based test, you will NOT be able to underline portions of reading passages, write on diagrams of geometry figures, or otherwise physically mark up problems. So get used to this now. Solve the problems in these books on scratch paper. (Each of our books talks specifically about what to write down for different problem types).

Again, as you study stay focused on the test-day experience. As you progress, work on timed drills and sets of questions. Eventually, you should be taking full practice tests (available at www.manhattangre.com) under realistic timed conditions.

Changes to the Exam

Finally, you've probably heard that the GRE is changing in August, 2011. Look in the back of this book for more information about the switch—every one of these GRE books contains additional material for the 2011 GRE, and we'll be constantly updating www.manhattangre.com as new information becomes available. If you're going to take the test before the changeover, it's nothing to worry about.

Diving In

While we love standardized tests, we understand that your goal is really about grad school, and your life beyond that. However, you'll make your way through these books much more easily—and much more pleasantly—if you can stay positive and engaged throughout. Hopefully, the process of studying for the GRE will make your brain a more interesting place to be! Now let's get started!

TABLE OF CONTENTS

Chapter 1
of
WORD TRANSLATIONS

WORD
PROBLEMS

In This Chapter . . .

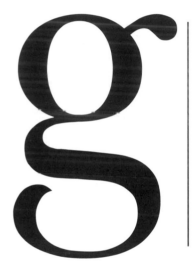

- Decoding the GRE Word Problem
- Common Word Problem Phrases
- Translating Word Correctly
- Hidden Constraints

WORD PROBLEMS

In This Chapter:

- Understanding what word problems are asking
- Translating word problems into equations

Decoding the GRE Word Problem

Two thoughts are common to many frustrated students:

"I don't know where to get started" and "I don't know what they want me to do."

Let's attack these frustrations one at a time.

"I don't know where to get started."

A *passive thinker* takes in information, hopes that it will lead somewhere, waits for a connection to appear and then… (hopefully)… *voila!* In contrast, the *active thinker* aggressively seeks out relationships between the various elements of a problem and looks to write equations which can be solved. *You have to be an active thinker on the GRE.*

Let's look at a sample problem:

> A steel rod 50 meters long is cut into two pieces. If one piece is 14 meters longer than the other, what is the length, in meters, of the shorter piece?

The trick to word problems is to not try to do everything all at once. While it's great when the entire process is clear from the start, such clarity about your work is often not the case. That's why **we need to start by identifying unknowns and creating variables.** What quantities have we not been given specific values for? Take a moment to identify those quantities and write them down in the space provided below. Make up letters to stand for the quantities, and label these letters.

Identify Unknowns and create variables

In this question, both the length of the shorter piece and the length of the longer piece are unknown, so let's begin by assigning each of those values a variable. We could go with the traditional algebraic variables x and y, but what if we forget which is which while we're busy answering the question? Instead, let's use letters that can help us remember which variable is assigned to which value:

S = shorter piece
L = longer piece

Just like that, we've gotten started on this problem. This may seem like a minor accomplishment in terms of the entire question, but it was an important one. Often, as soon as you start translating a word problem, the path forward becomes clearer. Now it's time to deal with our second frustration.

"I don't know what they want me to do."

Even now that we've identified and labeled our variables, you might still feel confused. That's fine. Since the GRE is computer-adaptive, everyone ends up facing a number of problems that are above his or her ability level. What distinguishes the higher performing GRE test-takers in these moments is that they begin spelling out relationships before they know how the equations will prove useful. It's similar to untangling a ball of yarn: if you waited until you knew how the entire process would end, you might never get started. Of course, you hope to have a clear vision right from the start, but if you don't, dive in and see what you find—you'll likely make key realizations along the way. Ironically, often it's the road blocks we encounter that point the way. So our next step is to **identify relationships and create equations.**

Let's go back to our problem, look at one piece of information at a time, and start translating that information into equations. Try it first on your own, then we'll go through it together.

A steel rod 50 meters long is cut into two pieces.

The relationship expressed here is one of the two most common types of relationships found in word problems. We know the original length of the rod was 50 meters, and we know that it was cut into 2 pieces. Therefore, we know that the length of the shorter piece plus the length of the longer piece must equal 50 meters. This common relationship (one you should watch out for in other word problems) is **Parts Add to a Sum**. So a good way to express this relationship algebraically would be to write

$S + L = 50$

Now that we've translated the first part of the problem, let's move on to the next part.

If one piece is 14 meters longer than the other...

The relationship expressed here is another common type found in word problems. The longer piece of metal is 14 meters longer than the shorter piece of metal. So if we were to add 14 meters to the shorter piece, it would be the same length as the longer piece. This relationship (be on the lookout for this one too) is **One Part Can Be Made Equal to the Other**. Either the question will say that two values are equivalent, or it will tell you exactly how they differ. This question told us how they were different, so our equation shows how we could make them equivalent. In this case, we would want to say

$S + 14 = L$

By the way, when constructing equations in which you are making one part equal to the other, it can be very easy to express the relationship backwards. If you mistakenly wrote down $S = L + 14$, you're not alone.

A good habit to get into if you find yourself making this kind of error is to verify your equation with real, but hypothetical, numbers. To check if my equation above is correct, I'm going to start by imagining that my shorter piece of metal is 20 meters long. If the shorter piece were 20 meters long, then the longer piece would have to be 34 meters long. Now I plug those numbers into my equation. Does $(20) + 14 = (34)$? Yes, it does, so my equation is correct.

Let's move on to the final part of the question.

> *…what is the length, in meters, of the shorter piece?*

This part of the question doesn't describe a relationship that we can use to create an equation, but it does tell us something quite useful: it tells us what we're solving for! Make sure that you note in some way what value you're actually looking for as you solve a problem—it can help you stay focused on the task at hand. In this problem, we're trying to find *S*.

On your paper, you might even write

$$S = ?$$

So now that we've **identified** our **unknowns and created variables**, **identified relationships** and **created equations**, and **identified what the question is asking for**, it's time to put the pieces together and answer the question. Try it on your own first, and then when you've got an answer, turn the page and we'll go through the final steps together.

Let's recap, and then we'll complete the final steps and answer the question. After reading the question, we were able to create 2 equations:

$$S + L = 50$$
$$S + 14 = L$$

We've been in this situation before. We have 2 variables and 2 equations. It's time to solve for S.

$$S + L = 50 \;\rightarrow\; L = 50 - S$$

$$S + 14 = (50 - S)$$

$$\begin{aligned} S + 14 &= 50 - S \\ -14 \quad &\quad -14 \end{aligned}$$

$$\begin{aligned} S &= 36 - S \\ +S \quad &\quad +S \end{aligned}$$

$$\frac{2S}{2} = \frac{36}{2}$$
$$S = 18$$

If you had trouble getting the correct values for S and L, then you should probably go back and refresh your algebra skills (see our Algebra guide). Knowing how to substitute and solve is absolutely essential if you want to do consistently well on word problems. If you're comfortable with everything we've done so far in order to answer the question, then you're ready for a tougher problem.

> Jack is 13 years older than Ben. In 8 years, he will be twice as old as Ben. How old is Jack now?

First try this problem on your own. Remember to follow the same steps we followed in the last question. After you're finished, we'll go through it together on the next page.

Ok, let's get started. The first thing we have to do is **identify** our **unknowns** and **create variables**. In this problem, the two unknowns are the ages of Jack and Ben. We can represent them like this:

J = Jack's age NOW
B = Ben's age NOW

Before we move on to the next step, it's important to understand why we want to specify that our variables represent Jack and Ben's ages NOW. As you were solving this problem by yourself, you may have noticed that there was an added wrinkle to this question. We are presented with information that describes 2 distinct points in time—now and 8 years from now. Some word problems on the GRE provide information about 2 distinct but related situations. When you are dealing with one of those problems, be careful about the reference point for your variables. In this case, we want to say that our variables represent Jack and Ben's ages *now* as opposed to 8 years from now. This makes it easier to express their ages at other points in time.

Now that we've created our variables, it's time to **identify relationships** and **create equations**. Let's go through the information presented in the question one piece at a time.

Jack is 13 years older than Ben.

Once again, we should check that we're putting this together the right way (not putting the +13 on the wrong side of the equation). Our equation should be

$J = B + 13$, NOT $J + 13 = B$

Let's move on to the next piece of information.

In 8 years, he will be twice as old as Ben.

This piece is more challenging to translate than you might otherwise suspect. Remember, our variables represent their ages now, but this statement is talking about their ages 8 years from now. So we can't just write $J = 2B$. This relationship is dependent upon Jack and Ben's ages 8 years from now. We don't want to use new variables to represent these different ages, so let's adjust the values like this:

$(J + 8)$ = Jack's age 8 years from now
$(B + 8)$ = Ben's age 8 years from now

Now we can accurately create equations related to the earlier time *and* to the later time. Plus, if we keep those values in parentheses, then we can avoid potential PEMDAS errors! So our second equation really should read

$(J + 8) = 2(B + 8)$

Only one more piece of the question to go.

How old is Jack now?

This tells us that we're looking for the value of J. In other words, $J = ?$. All the pieces are in place and we're ready to solve.

$(J + 8) = 2(B + 8) \rightarrow J + 8 = 2B + 16$ Simplify grouped terms

$J = B + 13 \rightarrow J - 13 = B$ Isolate the variable you want to eliminate

$J + 8 = 2(J - 13) + 16$ Substitute into the other equation

$J + 8 = 2J - 26 + 16$ Simplify grouped terms

$$\begin{aligned} J + 8 &= 2J - 10 \\ -J + 10 \quad &\quad -J + 10 \\ \hline 18 &= J \end{aligned}$$

The question asks for Jack's age, so we have our answer. Let's review what we know about word problems and the steps we should take to solve them.

Step 1: Identify unknowns and create variables

- Don't forget to use descriptive letters (i.e. shorter piece = S).
- Be very specific when dealing with questions that contain 2 distinct but related situations (i.e. Jack's age NOW = J vs. Jack's age in 8 years = $J + 8$).

Step 2: Identify relationships and create equations

- As a general guideline, once you have identified how many variables you have, that will give you a big clue as to how many equations you will ultimately need. If you have 2 variables, you will need 2 equations to be able to find unique values for those variables.
- Don't forget to look at one piece of the question at a time. Don't try to do everything at once!
- Use numbers to check that you have set up your equation correctly. For example, if they say that Jack is twice as old as Ben, which is correct: $J = 2B$ or $2J = B$? If Jack were 40, Ben would be 20, so $(40) = 2(20)$ or $2(40) = 20$?

Step 3: Identify what the question is asking for

- Having a clear goal can prevent you from losing track of what you're doing and can help you stay focused on the task at hand.

Step 4: Solve for the wanted element (often by using substitution)

- The ability to perform every step accurately and efficiently is critical to success on the GRE—practice makes perfect!

Now that we've gone through the basic steps, it's time to practice translating word problems into equations. But first, here are some common mathematical relationships found on the GRE, words and phrases you might find used to describe them, and their translations. Use them to help you with the drill sets at the end of this chapter.

Common Word Problem Phrases

Addition
Add, Sum, Total(of parts), More Than: +
The sum of x and y: $x + y$
The sum of the three funds combined: $a + b + c$
When fifty is added to his age: $a + 50$
Six pounds heavier than Dave: $d + 6$
A group of men and women: $m + w$
The cost is marked up: $c + m$

Subtraction
Minus, Difference, Less Than: −
x minus five: $x - 5$
The difference between Quentin's and Rachel's heights (if Quentin is taller): $q - r$
Four pounds less than expected: $e - 4$
The profit is the revenue minus the cost: $P = R - C$

Multiplication
The product of h and k: $h \times k$
The number of reds times the number of blues: $r \times b$
One fifth of y: $(1/5) \times y$
n persons have x beads each: total number of beads $= nx$
Go z miles per hour for t hours: distance $= zt$ miles

Ratios and Division
Quotient, Per, Ratio, Proportion: ÷ or /
Five dollars every two weeks: (5 dollars/2 weeks) → 2.5 dollars a week
The ratio of x to y: x/y
The proportion of girls to boys: g/b

Average or Mean (sum of terms divided by the total number of terms)

The average of a and b: $\dfrac{a+b}{2}$

The average salary of the three doctors: $\dfrac{x+y+z}{3}$

A student's average score on 5 tests was 87: $\dfrac{\text{sum}}{5} = 87$ or $\dfrac{a+b+c+d+e}{5} = 87$

Translating Words Correctly

Avoid writing relationships backwards.

If You See...		Write		Not
"A is half the size of B"	✓	$A = \dfrac{1}{2}B$	✗	$B = \dfrac{1}{2}A$
"A is 5 less than B"	✓	$A = B - 5$	✗	$A = 5 - B$
"A is less than B"	✓	$A < B$	✗	$A > B$
"Jane bought twice as many apples as bananas"	✓	$A = 2B$	✗	$2A = B$

Quickly check your translation with easy numbers.

For the last example above, you might think the following:

> "Jane bought twice as many apples as bananas. More apples than bananas. Say she buys 5 bananas. She buys twice as many apples—that's 10 apples. Makes sense. So the equation is Apples equals 2 times Bananas, or $A = 2B$, not the other way around."

These numbers do not have to satisfy any other conditions of the problem. Use these "quick picks" only to test the form of your translation.

Write an unknown percent as a variable divided by 100.

If You See...		Write		Not
"P is X percent of Q"	✓	$P = \dfrac{X}{100}Q$ or $\dfrac{P}{Q} = \dfrac{X}{100}$	✗	$P = X\%Q$ (cannot be manipulated)

Translate bulk discounts and similar relationships carefully.

If You See...		Write		Not
"Pay $10 per CD for the first 2 CDs, then $7 per additional CD"	✓	n = # of CDs bought T = total amount paid ($) $T = \$10 \times 2 + \$7 \times (n - 2)$ (assuming $n > 2$)	✗	$T = \$10 \times 2 + \$7 \times n$

Always pay attention to the *meaning* of the sentence you are translating!

Check Your Skills

Translate the following statements:

1. Lily is two years older than Melissa.
2. A small pizza costs $5 less than a large pizza.
3. Twice *A* is 5 more than *B*.
4. *R* is 45 percent of *Q*.
5. John has more than twice as many CDs as Ken.

Answers may be found on page 23.

Hidden Constraints

Notice that in some problems, there is a **hidden constraint** on the possible quantities. This would apply, for instance, to the number of apples and bananas that Jane bought. Since each fruit is a physical, countable object, you can only have a **whole number** of each type. Whole numbers are the integers 0, 1, 2, and so on. So you can have 1 apples, 2 apples, 3 apples, etc., and even 0 apples, but you cannot have fractional apples or negative apples.

As a result of this implied "whole number" constraint, you often have more information than you might think and you may be able to answer a question with fewer facts.

Consider the following example:

> If Kelly received 1/3 more votes than Mike in a student election, which of the following could have been the total number of votes cast for the two candidates?
>
> (A) 12   (B) 13   (C) 14   (D) 15   (E) 16

Let *M* be the number of votes cast for Mike. Then Kelly received $M + (1/3)M$, or $(4/3)M$ votes. The total number of votes cast was therefore "votes for Mike" plus "votes for Kelly," or $M + (4/3)M$. This quantity equals $(7/3)M$, or $7M/3$.

Because *M* is a number of votes, it cannot be a fraction—specifically, not a fraction with a 7 in the denominator. Therefore, the 7 in the expression $7M/3$ cannot be cancelled out. As a result, the total number of votes cast must be a multiple of 7. Among the answer choices, the only multiple of 7 is 14, so the correct answer is (**C**).

Another way to solve this problem is this: the number of votes cast for Mike (*M*) must be a multiple of 3, since the total number of votes is a whole number. So $M = 3, 6, 9$, etc. Kelly received 1/3 more votes, so the number of votes she received is 4, 8, 12, etc. Thus the total number of votes is 7, 14, 21, etc.

Not every unknown quantity related to real objects is restricted to whole numbers. Many physical measurements, such as weights, times, or speeds, can be any positive number, not necessarily integers. A few quantities can even be negative (e.g., temperatures, *x*- or *y*-coordinates). Think about what is being measured or counted, and you will recognize whether a hidden constraint applies.

Check Your Skills

Translate the following statements:

6. In a certain word, the number of consonants is 1/4 more than the number of vowels. Which of the following is a possibility for the number of letters in the word?

   (A) 8   (B) 9   (C) 10   (D) 11   (E) 12

Answers may be found on page 23.

Check Your Skills Answers

1. $L = M + 2$

2. $S = L - 5$

3. $2A = B + 5$

4. $R = \dfrac{45}{100} \cdot Q$ or $R = 0.45Q$

5. $J > 2K$

6. **(B) 9:** There is a hidden constraint in this question. The number of vowels and the number of consonants must both be integers. The number of consonants is 1/4 more than the number of vowels, which means we need to multiply the number of vowels by 1/4 to determine how many more consonants there are. If we label the number of vowels v, then there are $v/4$ more consonants than vowels. The only way that $v/4$ will be an integer is if v is a multiple of 4.

If $v = 4$, there is $(4)/4 = 1$ more consonant than there are vowels, so there are $4 + 1 = 5$ consonants. That gives a total of $4 + 5 = 9$ letters in the word. The correct answer is B.

Problem Set

Solve the following problems with the four-step method outlined in this section.

1.   John is 20 years older than Brian. 12 years ago, John was twice as old as Brian. How old is Brian?

2.   Mrs. Miller has two dogs, Jackie and Stella, who weigh a total of 75 pounds. If Stella weighs 15 pounds less than twice Jackie's weight, how much does Stella weigh?

3.   Caleb spends $72.50 on 50 hamburgers for the marching band. If single burgers cost $1.00 each and double burgers cost $1.50 each, how many double burgers did he buy?

4.   United Telephone charges a base rate of $10.00 for service, plus an additional charge of $0.25 per minute. Atlantic Call charges a base rate of $12.00 for service, plus an additional charge of $0.20 per minute. For what number of minutes would the bills for each telephone company be the same?

5.   Carla cuts a 70-inch piece of ribbon into 2 pieces. If the first piece is five inches more than one fourth as long as the second piece, how long is the longer piece of ribbon?

6.   Jane started baby-sitting when she was 18 years old. Whenever she baby-sat for a child, that child was no more than half her age at the time. Jane is currently 32 years old, and she stopped baby-sitting 10 years ago. What is the current age of the oldest person for whom Jane could have baby-sat?

7.

Ten years ago, Brian was twice as old as Aubrey.

Column A	**Column B**
Twice Aubrey's age today	Brian's age today

8.

The length of a rectangular room is 8 feet greater than its width. The total area of the room is 240 square feet.

Column A	**Column B**
The width of the room in feet	12

9.

John earns a yearly base salary of $30,000, plus a commission of $500 on every car he sells above his monthly minimum of two cars. Last year, John met or surpassed his minimum sales every month, and earned a total income (salary plus commission) of $60,000.

Column A	Column B
The number of cars John sold last year	90

1. 32: Use an age chart to assign variables. Represent Brian's age now with b. Then John's age now is $b + 20$.

	12 years ago	Now
John	$b + 8$	$b + 20$
Brian	$b - 12$	$b = ?$

Subtract 12 from the "now" column to get the "12 years ago" column.

Then write an equation to represent the remaining information: 12 years ago, John was twice as old as Brian. Solve for b:

$$b + 8 = 2(b - 12)$$
$$b + 8 = 2b - 24$$
$$32 = b$$

You could also solve this problem by inspection. John is 20 years older than Brian. We also need John to be *twice* Brian's age at a particular point in time. Since John is always 20 years older, then he must be 40 years old at that time (and Brian must be 20 years old). This point in time was 12 years ago, so Brian is now 32 years old.

2. 45 pounds:

Let j = Jackie's weight, and let s = Stella's weight. Stella's weight is the Ultimate Unknown: $s = ?$

The two dogs weigh a total of 75 pounds.   Stella weighs 15 pounds less than twice Jackie's weight.
$$j + s = 75 \qquad\qquad\qquad s = 2j - 15$$

Combine the two equations by substituting the value for s from equation (2) into equation (1).
$$j + (2j - 15) = 75$$
$$3j - 15 = 75$$
$$3j = 90$$
$$j = 30$$

Find Stella's weight by substituting Jackie's weight into equation (1).
$$30 + s = 75$$
$$s = 45$$

3. 45 double burgers:

Let s = the number of single burgers purchased
Let d = the number of double burgers purchased

Caleb bought 50 burgers: Caleb spent \$72.50 in all:
$$s + d = 50 \qquad\qquad\qquad s + 1.5d = 72.50$$

Combine the two equations by subtracting equation (1) from equation (2).
$$
\begin{array}{r}
s + 1.5d = 72.50 \\
-(s + d = 50) \\
\hline
0.5d = 22.5 \\
d = 45
\end{array}
$$

4. **40 minutes:**
Let x = the number of minutes
A call made by United Telephone costs \$10.00 plus \$0.25 per minute: $10 + 0.25x$.
A call made by Atlantic Call costs \$12.00 plus \$0.20 per minute: $12 + 0.20x$.

Set the expressions equal to each other:
$$10 + 0.25x = 12 + 0.20x$$
$$0.05x = 2$$
$$x = 40$$

5. **52 inches:**

Let x = the 1st piece of ribbon
Let y = the 2nd piece of ribbon

The ribbon is 70 inches long.   The 1st piece is 5 inches more than 1/4 as long as the 2nd.

$$x + y = 70$$ $$x = 5 + \frac{y}{4}$$

Combine the equations by substituting the value of x from equation (2) into equation (1):

$$5 + \frac{y}{4} + y = 70$$
$$20 + y + 4y = 280$$
$$5y = 260$$
$$y = 52$$ Now, since $x + y = 70$, $x = 18$. This tells us that $x < y$, so y is the answer.

6. **23:** Since you are given actual ages for Jane, the easiest way to solve the problem is to think about the extreme scenarios. At one extreme, 18-year-old Jane could have baby-sat a child of age 9. Since Jane is now 32, that child would now be 23. At the other extreme, 22-year-old Jane could have baby-sat a child of age 11. Since Jane is now 32 that child would now be 21. We can see that the first scenario yields the oldest possible current age (23) of a child that Jane baby-sat.

7. **A:** Let A and B denote Aubrey and Brian's ages today. Then, their ages 10 years ago would be given by $A - 10$ and $B - 10$, respectively. Those ages are related by the problem statement as:

$$B - 10 = 2(A - 10)$$

Expanding and simplifying yields

$$B - 10 = 2A - 20$$
$$B = 2A - 10$$

Rewrite the columns in terms of A and B. Twice Aubrey's age today is $2A$ and Brian's age today is B.

Ten years ago, Brian was twice
as old as Aubrey.

Column A	**Column B**
Twice Aubrey's age today = 2A	Brian's age today = B

According to the equation, B is 10 less than $2A$. Therefore the value in Column A is larger.

8. **C:** Let L and W stand for the length and width of the room in feet. Then, from the first relation, we can write this equation:

$$L = W + 8$$

Moreover, the area of a rectangle is given by length times width, such that:

$$LW = 240$$

Taken together, we have two equations with two unknowns, and because the question involves the width rather than the length, we should eliminate the length by substituting from the first equation into the second:

$$(W + 8)W = 240$$

We can now expand the product and move everything to the left hand side, so that we may solve the quadratic equation by factoring it. This gives:

$$W^2 + 8W = 240$$
$$W^2 + 8W - 240 = 0$$
$$(W + 20)(W - 12) = 0$$

The two solutions are $W = -20$ and $W = 12$. A negative width does not make sense, so W must equal 12 feet.

It is also possible to arrive at the answer by testing the value in column B as the width of the room. Plug in 12 for W in the first equation

$$L = (12) + 8 = 20 \text{ feet}$$

If $W = 12$ and $L = 20$, then the area is $(20)(12) = 240$ square feet. Because this agrees with the given fact, we may conclude that 12 feet is indeed the width of the room.

Either method arrives at the conclusion that the values in both columns are equal.

9. **B:** The simplest method for solving a problem like this is to work backwards from the value in Column B. Suppose John sold exactly 90 cars. Then, since he met or surpassed his minimum sales each month (which add up to 24 cars in the entire year), he would have sold another $90 - 24 = 66$ cars above the minimum.

The commission he earned on those cars is calculated as follows:

$500 × 66 = $33,000

This would put his total yearly income at $30,000 (base salary) + $33,000 (commission) = $63,000. However, we know that John actually earned less than that; therefore, he must have sold fewer than 90 cars.

Column A	**Column B**
The number of cars John sold last year = less than 90	90

The alternative approach is to translate John's total earnings into an algebraic expression. Suppose John sold N cars. Once again, noting that he met or surpassed his monthly minimum sales, we would need to subtract 24 cars that do not contribute to his bonus from this total, and then solve for N as follows:

$$\$60,000 = \$30,000 + \$500 \times (N - 24)$$
$$\$30,000 = \$500 \times (N - 24)$$
$$60 = N - 24$$
$$84 = N$$

Chapter 2
of
WORD TRANSLATIONS

RATES & WORK

In This Chapter . . .

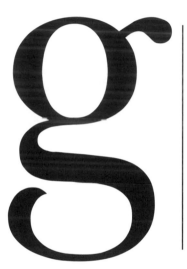

- Basic Motion: The RTD Chart
- Matching Units in the RTD
- Average Rate: Don't Just Add and Divide
- Basic Work Problems
- Population Problems

RATES & WORK

The GRE's favorite Word Translation type is the RATE problem. Rate problems come in a variety of forms on the GRE, but all are marked by three primary components: RATE, TIME, & DISTANCE or WORK.

These three elements are related by the equation:

Rate × Time = Distance

or   **Rate × Time = Work**

These equations can be abbreviated as $RT = D$ or as $RT = W$. Basic rate problems involve simple manipulations of these equations.

Note that rate-of-travel problems (with a physical distance) and work problems are really the same from the point of view of the math. The main difference is that for work problems, the right side of the equation is not a distance but an *output* (e.g., hamburgers cooked). Also, the rate is measured not in units of distance per unit of time (e.g., 10 miles per hour), but in units of *output* per unit of time (e.g., 5 hamburgers cooked per minute).

Rate problems on the GRE come in four main forms:

(1)   Basic Motion Problems
(2)   Average Rate Problems
(3)   Work Problems
(4)   Population Problems

Basic Motion: The RTD Chart

All basic motion problems involve three elements: Rate, Time, and Distance.

Rate is expressed as a ratio of distance and time, with two corresponding units.
Some examples of rates include: 30 miles per hour, 10 meters/second, 15 kilometers/day.

Time is expressed using a unit of time.
Some examples of times include: 6 hours, 23 seconds, 5 months, etc.

Distance is expressed using a unit of distance.
Some examples of distances include: 18 miles, 20 meters, 100 kilometers.

You can make an "RTD chart" to solve a basic motion problem. Read the problem and fill in two of the variables. Then use the $RT = D$ formula to find the missing variable.

   If a car is traveling at 30 miles per hour, how long does it take to travel 75 miles?

An RTD chart is shown to the right. Fill in your RTD chart with the given information. Then solve for the time:

$30t = 75$, or $t = 2.5$ hours

	Rate (mi/hr)	×	Time (hr)	=	Distance (mi)
Car	30 mi/hr	×	t (hr)	=	75 mi

Matching Units in the RTD Chart

All the units in your RTD chart must match up with one another. The two units in the rate should match up with the unit of time and the unit of distance.

For example:

> It takes an elevator four seconds to go up one floor. How many floors will the elevator rise in two minutes?

The rate is 1 floor/4 seconds, which simplifies to 0.25 floors/second. Note: the rate is NOT 4 seconds per floor! This is an extremely frequent error. **Always express rates as "distance over time,"** not as "time over distance."

The time is 2 minutes. The distance is unknown.

	R (floors/sec)	×	T (min)	=	W (floors)
Elevator	0.25	×	2	=	?

Watch out! There is a problem with this RTD chart. The rate is expressed in floors per second, but the time is expressed in minutes. This will yield an incorrect answer.

To correct this table, we change the time into seconds. Then all the units will match.

	R (floors/sec)	×	T (sec)	=	W (floors)
Elevator	0.25	×	120	=	?

Once the time has been converted from 2 minutes to 120 seconds, the time unit will match the rate unit, and we can solve for the distance using the $RT = D$ equation:

$$0.25(120) = d \qquad d = 30 \text{ floors}$$

Another example:

> A train travels 90 kilometers/hr. How many hours does it take the train to travel 450,000 meters?

Before entering the information into the RTD chart, we convert the distance from 450,000 meters to 450 km. This matches the distance unit with the rate unit (kilometers per hour).

	R (km/hr)	×	T (hr)	=	W (km)
Train	90	×	?	=	450

We can now solve for the time: $90t = 450$. Thus, $t = 5$ hours.
Note that this time is the "stopwatch" time: if you started a stopwatch at the start of the trip, what would the stopwatch read at the end of the trip? This is not what a clock on the wall would read, but if you take the *difference* of the start and end clock times (say, 1 pm and 6 pm), you will get the stopwatch time of 5 hours.

The RTD chart may seem like overkill for relatively simple problems such as these. In fact, for such problems, you can simply set up the equation $RT = D$ or $RT = W$ and then substitute. However, the RTD chart comes into its own when we have more complicated scenarios that contain more than one RTD relationship, as we see in the next section.

Check Your Skills

1. Convert 10 meters per second to meters per hour.
2. It takes an inlet pipe 2 minutes to supply 30 gallons of water to a pool. How many hours will it take to fill a 27,000 gallon pool that starts out empty?

Answers can be found on page 39.

Average Rate: Don't Just Add and Divide

Consider the following problem:

> If Lucy walks to work at a rate of 4 miles per hour, but she walks home by the same route at a rate of 6 miles per hour, what is Lucy's average walking rate for the round trip?

It is very tempting to find an average rate as you would find any other average: add and divide. Thus, you might say that Lucy's average rate is 5 miles per hour (4 + 6 = 10 and 10 ÷ 2 = 5). However, this is INCORRECT!

If an object moves the **same distance** twice, but at **different rates**, then *the average rate will NEVER be the average of the two rates given for the two legs of the journey*. In fact, because the object spends more time traveling at the slower rate, *the average rate will be closer to the slower of the two rates than to the faster*.

In order to find the average rate, you must first find the TOTAL combined time for the trips and the TOTAL combined distance for the trips.

First, we need a value for the distance. Since all we need to know to determine the average rate is the *total time* and *total distance*, we can actually pick any number for the distance. The portion of the total distance represented by each part of the trip ("Going" and "Return") will dictate the time.

Pick a Smart Number for the distance. Since you would like to choose a multiple of the two rates in the problem, 4 and 6, 12 is an ideal choice.

Set up a Multiple RTD Chart:

	Rate (mi/hr)	×	Time (hr)	=	Distance (mi)
Going	4 mi/hr	×		=	12 mi
Return	6 mi/hr	×		=	12 mi
Total	?	×		=	24 mi

The times can be found using the *RTD* equation. For the GOING trip, $4t = 12$, so $t = 3$ hrs. For the RETURN trip, $6t = 12$, so $t = 2$ hrs. Thus, the total time is 5 hrs.

	Rate (mi/hr)	×	Time (hr)	=	Distance (mi)
Going	4 mi/hr	×	**3 hrs**	=	12 mi
Return	6 mi/hr	×	**2 hrs**	=	12 mi
Total	?	×	**5 hrs**	=	24 mi

Now that we have the total Time and the total Distance, we can find the Average Rate using the RTD formula:

$$RT = D$$
$$r(5) = 24$$
$$r = 4.8 \text{ miles per hour}$$

Again, 4.8 miles per hour is *not* the simple average of 4 miles per hour and 6 miles per hour. In fact, it is the weighted average of the two rates, with the *times* as the weights. Because of that, the average rate is closer to the slower of the two rates.

You can test different numbers for the distance (try 24 or 36) to prove that you will get the same answer, regardless of the number you choose for the distance.

Check Your Skills

3. Juan bikes halfway to school at 9 miles per hour, and walks the rest of the distance at 3 miles per hour. What is Juan's average speed for the whole trip?

Answer can be found on page 39.

Basic Work Problems

Work problems are just another type of rate problem. Just like all other rate problems, work problems involve three elements: rate, time, and "distance."

WORK: In work problems, distance is replaced by work, which refers to the number of jobs completed or the number of items produced.

TIME: This is the time spent working.

RATE: In motion problems, the rate is a ratio of distance to time, or the amount of distance traveled in one time unit. In work problems, the rate is a ratio of work to time, or the amount of work completed in one time unit.

Figuring Work Rates

Work rates usually include one major twist not seen in distance problems: you often have to *calculate* the work rate.

In distance problems, if the rate (speed) is known, it will normally be *given* to you as a ready-to-use number. In work problems, though, you will usually have to *figure out* the rate from some given information about how many jobs the agent can complete in a given amount of time:

$$\text{Work rate} = \frac{\text{Given \# of jobs}}{\text{Given amount of time}} \text{, or } \frac{1}{\text{Time to complete 1 job}}$$

For instance, if Oscar can perform one hand surgery in 1.5 hours, his work rate is

$$\frac{1 \text{ operation}}{1.5 \text{ hours}} = \frac{2}{3} \text{ operation per hour}$$

Remember the rate is NOT 1.5 hours per hand surgery! **Always express work rates as jobs per unit time, not as time per job.** Also, you need to distinguish this type of general information—which is meant to specify the work <u>rate</u>—from the data given about the actual work performed, or the time required to perform that specific work.

For example:

> If a copier can make 3 copies every 2 seconds, how long will it take to make 40 copies?

Here, the work is 40 copies, because this is the number of items that will be produced. The time is unknown. The rate is 3 copies/2 seconds, or 1.5 copies per second. Notice the use of the verb "can" with the general rate.

> If it takes Anne 5 hours to paint one fence, and she has been working for 7 hours, how many fences has she painted?

Here the time is 7 hours, because that is the time which Anne spent working. The work done is unknown. Anne's general working rate is 1 fence per 5 hours, or 1/5 fence per hour. Be careful: her rate is not 5 hours per fence, but rather 0.2 fence per hour. Again, always express rates as work per time unit, not time per work unit. Also, notice that the "5 hours" is part of the general rate, whereas the "7 hours" is the actual time for this specific situation. Distinguish the general description of the work rate from the specific description of the episode or task. Here is a useful test: you should be able to add the phrase "in general" to the rate information. For example, we can easily imagine the following:

> If, <u>in general</u>, a copier can make 3 copies every 2 seconds…

> If, <u>in general</u>, it takes Anne 5 hours to paint one fence…

Since the insertion of "in general" makes sense, we know that these parts of the problem contain the general rate information.

Basic work problems are solved like basic rate problems, using an RTW chart or the RTW equation. Simply replace the distance with the work. They can also be solved with a simple proportion. Here are both methods for Anne's work problem:

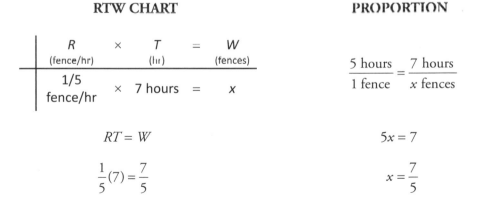

Anne has painted 7/5 of a fence, or 1.4 fences. Note that you can set up the proportion either as "hours/fence" or as "fences/hour." You must simply be consistent on both sides of the equation. However, any rate in an $RT = W$ relationship must be in "fences/hour." (Verify for yourself that the answer to the copier problem above is 80/3 seconds or 26 2/3 seconds.)

Check Your Skills

4. Sophie can address 20 envelopes in one hour. How long will it take her to address 50 envelopes?
5. If a steel mill can produce 1500 feet of I-beams every 20 minutes, how many feet of I-beams can it produce in 50 minutes?

Answers can be found on page 39.

Population Problems

The final type of rate problem on the GRE is the population problem. In such problems, some population typically increases <u>by a common factor</u> every time period. These can be solved with a Population Chart.

Consider the following example:

> The population of a certain type of bacterium triples every 10 minutes. If the population of a colony 20 minutes ago was 100, in approximately how many minutes from now will the bacteria population reach 24,000?

You can solve simple population problems, such as this one, by using a Population Chart. Make a table with a few rows, labeling one of the middle rows as "NOW." Work forward, backward, or both (as necessary in the problem), obeying any conditions given in the problem statement about the rate of growth or decay. In this case, simply triple each population number as you move down a row. Notice that while the population increases by a constant <u>factor</u>, it does <u>not</u> increase by a constant <u>amount</u> each time period.

For this problem, the Population Chart below shows that the bacterial population will reach 24,000 about 30 minutes from now.

In some cases, you might pick a Smart Number for a starting point in your Population Chart. If you do so, pick a number that makes the computations as simple as possible.

Time Elapsed	Population
20 minutes ago	100
10 minutes ago	300
NOW	900
in 10 minutes	2,700
in 20 minutes	8,100
in 30 minutes	24,300

Check Your Skills

6. The population of amoebas in a colony doubles every two days. If there were 200 amoebas in the colony six days ago, how many amoebas will there be four days from now?

Answer can be found on page 40.

Check Your Skills Answers

1. **36,000 meters/hour:** First convert seconds to minutes. There are 60 seconds in a minute, so 10 m/sec × 60 = 600 m/min.

Now convert minutes to hours. There are 60 minutes in 1 hour, so 600 m/min × 60 = 36,000 m/hr.

2. **30 hours:** First simplify the rate. $R = \dfrac{30 \text{ gal}}{2 \text{ min}} = \dfrac{15 \text{ gal}}{1 \text{ min}}$, which is the same as 15 gal/min. The question

asks for the number of hours it will take to fill the pool, so convert minutes to hours. There are 60 minutes in an hour, so the rate is 15 gal/min × 60 = 900 gal/hr. Now we can set up an RTW chart. Let t be the time it takes to fill the pool.

	R (gal/hr)	×	T (hr)	=	W (gallons)
inlet pipe	900	×	t	=	27,000

$900t = 27,000$
$t = 30$

3. **4.5 mph:** Assume a Smart Number for the total distance. The Smart number should be divisible by two (since we are interested in half the distance), and each half should be divisible by 9 and 3. The simplest choice is 18 miles for the total distance.

> Time biking: $T = D/R = 9/9 = 1$ hr
> Time walking: $T = D/R = 9/3 = 3$ hr
> Total Time: 1 hr + 3 hr = 4 hr
>
> Average Speed $= \dfrac{\text{Total Distance}}{\text{Total Time}} = \dfrac{18 \text{ miles}}{4 \text{ hours}} = 4.5$ mph

4. **2.5 hours:** If she addresses 20 envelopes in 1 hour, then the rate at which she addresses is 20 envelopes/hr. we can set up an RTW equation.

> 20 envelopes/hr $\times T = 50$ envelopes
> $T = 50 / 20 = 2.5$ hr

5. **3,750 feet:** The rate at which the steel mill produces I-beams is $\dfrac{1500 \text{ ft}}{20 \text{ min}} = 75$ ft/min . We can set up an

RTW equation. Let w represent the number of feet of I-beam produced:

> 75 ft/min × 50 min = w
> 3750 ft = w

6. **6400:**

Time	Population
6 days ago	200
4 days ago (Careful! Count by two days.)	400
2 days ago	800
NOW	1,600
2 days from now	3,200
4 days from now	6,400

Problem Set

Solve the following problems, using the strategies you have learned in this section. Use RTD or RTW charts as appropriate to organize information.

1. A cat travels at 60 inches/second. How long will it take this cat to travel 300 feet? (12 inches = 1 foot)

2. Water is being poured into a tank at the rate of approximately 4 cubic feet per hour. If the tank is 6 feet long, 4 feet wide, and 8 feet deep, how many hours will it take to fill up the tank?

3. The population of grasshoppers doubles in a particular field every year. Approximately how many years will it take the population to grow from 2,000 grasshoppers to 1,000,000 or more?

4. An empty bucket being filled with paint at a constant rate takes 6 minutes to be filled to 7/10 of its capacity. How much more time will it take to fill the bucket to full capacity?

5. 4 years from now, the population of a colony of bees will reach 1.6×10^8. If the population of the colony doubles every 2 years, what was the population 4 years ago?

6. The Technotronic can produce 5 bad songs per hour. Wanting to produce bad songs more quickly, the record label also buys a Wonder Wheel, which works as fast as the Technotronic. Working together, how many bad songs can the two produce in 72 minutes?

7. Jack is putting together gift boxes at a rate of 3 per hour in the first hour. Then Jill comes over and yells, "Work faster!" Jack, now nervous, works at the rate of only 2 gift boxes per hour for the next 2 hours. Then Alexandra comes to Jack and whispers, "The steadiest hand is capable of the divine." Jack, calmer, then puts together 5 gift boxes in the fourth hour. What is the average rate at which Jack puts together gift boxes over the entire period?

8.

Hector can solve one word problem every 4 minutes before noon, and one word problem every 10 minutes after noon.

<table>
<tr><td><u>Column A</u></td><td><u>Column B</u></td></tr>
<tr><td>The number of word problems Hector can solve between 11:40am and noon</td><td>The number of word problems Hector can solve between noon and 12:40pm</td></tr>
</table>

9.

The number of users (non-zero) of a social networking website doubles every 4 months.

Column A

Ten times the number of users one year ago

Column B

The number of users today

10.

A bullet train can cover the 420 kilometers between Xenia and York at a rate of 240 kilometers per hour.

Column A

The number of minutes it will take the train to travel from Xenia to York

Column B

100

1. **1 minute:** This is a simple application of the $RT = D$ formula, involving one unit conversion. First convert the rate, 60 inches/second, into 5 feet/second (given that 12 inches = 1 foot). Substitute this value for R. Substitute the distance, 300 feet, for D. Then solve:

$$(5 \text{ ft/s})(t) = 300 \text{ ft}$$

$$t = \frac{300 \text{ ft}}{5 \text{ ft/s}} = 60 \text{ seconds} = 1 \text{ minute}$$

	R (ft/sec)	×	T (sec)	=	D (ft)
	5	×	t	=	300

2. **48 hours:** The capacity of the tank is $6 \times 4 \times 8$, or 192 cubic feet. Use the $RT = W$ equation, substituting the rate, 4 ft³/hour, for R, and the capacity, 192 cubic feet, for W.

	R (ft³/hr)	×	T (hr)	=	W (ft³)
	4	×	t	=	192

$$(4 \text{ cubic feet/hr})(t) = 192 \text{ cubic feet}$$

$$t = \frac{192 \text{ cubic feet}}{4 \text{ cubic feet/hr}} = 48 \text{ hours}$$

3. **9 years:** Organize the information given in a population chart. Notice that since the population is increasing exponentially, it does not take very long for the population to top 1,000,000.

Time Elapsed	Population
NOW	2,000
1 year	4,000
2 years	8,000
3 years	16,000
4 years	32,000
5 years	64,000
6 years	128,000
7 years	256,000
8 years	512,000
9 years	1,024,000

4. $2\frac{4}{7}$ **minutes:** Use the $RT = W$ equation to solve for the rate, with $t = 6$ minutes and $w = 7/10$.

$$r(6 \text{ minutes}) = 7/10$$

$$r = 7/10 \div 6 = \frac{7}{60} \text{ buckets per minute.}$$

	R (bkt/min)	×	T (min)	=	W (bucket)
	r	×	6	=	7/10

Then, substitute this rate into the equation again, using 3/10 for w (the remaining work to be done).

$$\left(\frac{7}{60}\right)t = \frac{3}{10}$$

	R (bkt/min)	×	T (min)	=	W (bucket)
	7/60	×	t	=	3/10

$$t = \frac{3}{10} \div \frac{7}{60} = \frac{18}{7} = 2\frac{4}{7} \text{ minutes}$$

5. **1×10^7:** Organize the information given in a population chart.

Then, convert:
$$0.1 \times 10^8 = 10{,}000{,}000 = 1 \times 10^7 \text{ bees.}$$

Time Elapsed	Population
4 years ago	0.1×10^8
2 years ago	0.2×10^8
NOW	0.4×10^8
in 2 years	0.8×10^8
in 4 years	1.6×10^8

6. **12 songs:** Since this is a "working together" problem, add the individual rates: $5 + 5 = 10$ songs per hour.

The two machines together can produce 10 bad songs in 1 hour. Convert the given time into hours:

$$(72 \text{ minutes})\left(\frac{1 \text{ hour}}{60 \text{ minutes}}\right) = \frac{72}{60} = 1.2 \text{ hours}$$

	R (songs/hr)	×	T (hr)	=	W (songs)
	10	×	1.2	=	w

Then, use the $RT = W$ equation to find the total work done:

$$(10)(1.2 \text{ hours}) = w$$
$$w = 12 \text{ bad songs}$$

7. **3 boxes per hour:** The average rate is equal to the total work done divided by the time in which the work was done. Remember that you cannot simply average the rates. You must find the total work and total time. The total time is 4 hours. To find the total work, add up the boxes Jack put together in each hour: $3 + 2 + 2 + 5 = 12$. Therefore, the average rate is $\frac{12}{4}$, or 3 boxes per hour. The completed chart looks like this:

	R (box/hr)	×	T (hr)	=	W (box)
Phase 1	3	×	1	=	3
Phase 2	2	×	2	=	4
Phase 3	5	×	1	=	5
Total	3 = 12/4		4 Sum		12 Sum

8. **A:** This problem can be solved by an RTW chart or by a proportion. There are 20 minutes between 11:40am and noon, and 40 minutes between noon and 12:40pm. Hector's work rate is different for the two time periods. For the work period before noon, this is the proportion. Let *b* represent the number of problems Hector solves *before* noon.

$$\frac{b}{20 \text{ min}} = \frac{1 \text{ problem}}{4 \text{ min}}$$

$$4b = 20$$

$$b = 5$$

Let a represent the number of problems Hector solves *after* noon. The proportion can be written like this:

$$\frac{a}{40 \text{ min}} = \frac{1 \text{ problem}}{10 \text{ min}}$$

$$10a = 40$$

$$a = 4$$

Rewrite the columns:

Column A	**Column B**
The number of word problems Hector can solve between 11:40am and noon = 5	The number of word problems Hector can solve between noon and 12:40pm = 4

9. **A:** Set up a population chart, letting X denote the number of users one year ago:

Time	Number of users
12 months ago	X
8 months ago	$2X$
4 months ago	$4X$
NOW	$8X$

10 times the number of users one year ago is $10X$, while the number of users today is $8X$. Rewrite the columns:

The number of users (non-zero) of a social networking website doubles every 4 months.

Column A	**Column B**
Ten times the number of users one year ago = $10X$	The number of users today = $8X$

$10X$ is greater than $8X$ because X must be a positive number.

10. **A:** We can use the rate equation to solve for the time it will take the train to cover the distance. Our answer will be in hours because the given rate is in kilometers per hour. Let t stand for the total time of the trip.

$$R \times T = D$$
$$(240) \times t = (420)$$
$$t = \frac{420}{240} = \frac{7}{4}$$

(Note that we can omit the units in our calculation if we verify ahead of time that we are dealing with a consistent system of units.) Finally, we need to convert the time from hours into minutes: multiply $\frac{7}{4}$ by 60.

$$\frac{7}{4} \cdot 60 =$$

$$\frac{7}{1\,4} \cdot \cancel{60}^{15} =$$

105 minutes

Rewrite the columns:

A bullet train can cover the 420 kilometers between Xenia and York at a rate of 240 kilometers per hour.

Column A	**Column B**
The number of minutes it will take the train to travel from Xenia to York = 105	100

Alternately, you can use the value in Column B. Assume the train traveled for 100 minutes. Convert 100 minutes to hours:

$$\frac{100}{60} = \frac{5}{3} \text{ hours}$$

Now multiply the time ($\frac{5}{3}$ hours) by the rate (240 kilometers per hour) to calculate the distance.

$$D = \frac{5}{3} \cdot 240 =$$

$$\frac{5}{1\,3} \cdot \cancel{240}^{80} =$$

400 kilometers

The train can only travel 400 kilometers in 100 minutes, but the distance between the cities is 420 kilometers. Therefore, the train must have traveled longer than 100 minutes to reach its destination.

Chapter 3
of
WORD TRANSLATIONS

RATIOS

In This Chapter . . .

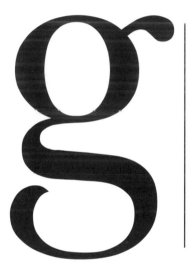

RATIOS

A ratio expresses a particular relationship between two or more quantities. Here are some examples of ratios:

> The two partners spend time working in the ratio of 1 to 3. For every 1 hour the first partner works, the second partner works 3 hours.

> Three sisters invest in a certain stock in the ratio of 2 to 3 to 8. For every $2 the first sister invests, the second sister invests $3, and the third sister invests $8.

> The ratio of men to women in the room is 3 to 4. For every 3 men, there are 4 women.

Ratios can be expressed in different ways:

> (1) Using the word "to," as in 3 to 4

> (2) Using a colon, as in 3 : 4

> (3) By writing a fraction, as in $\frac{3}{4}$ (only for ratios of 2 quantities)

Ratios can express a part–part relationship or a part–whole relationship:

> A part–part relationship: The ratio of men to women in the office is 3:4.
> A part–whole relationship: There are 3 men for every 7 employees.

Notice that if there are only two parts in the whole, you can derive a part–whole ratio from a part–part ratio, and vice versa.

The relationship that ratios express is division:

> If the ratio of men to women in the office is 3 : 4, then the number of men *divided by* the number of women equals $\frac{3}{4}$, or 0.75.

Remember that ratios only express a *relationship* between two or more items; they do not provide enough information, on their own, to determine the exact quantity for each item. For example, knowing that the ratio of men to women in an office is 3 to 4 does NOT tell us exactly how many men and how many women are in the office. All we know is that the number of men is $\frac{3}{4}$ the number of women.

If two quantities have a **constant ratio**, they are in direct proportion to each other.

> If the ratio of men to women in the office is 3 : 4, then $\dfrac{\text{\# of men}}{\text{\# of women}} = \dfrac{3}{4}$.

If the number of men is directly proportional to the number of women, then the number of men divided by the number of women is some constant.

Label Each Part of the Ratio with Units

The order in which a ratio is given is vital. For example, "the ratio of dogs to cats is 2 : 3" is very different from "the ratio of dogs to cats is 3 : 2." The first ratio says that for every 2 dogs, there are 3 cats. The second ratio says that for every 3 dogs, there are 2 cats.

It is very easy to accidentally reverse the order of a ratio—especially on a timed test like the GRE. Therefore, to avoid these reversals, always write units on either the ratio itself or the variables you create, or both.

Thus, if the ratio of dogs to cats is 2 : 3, you can write $\dfrac{x \text{ dogs}}{y \text{ cats}} = \dfrac{2 \text{ dogs}}{3 \text{ cats}}$, or simply $\dfrac{x \text{ dogs}}{y \text{ cats}} = \dfrac{2}{3}$, or even

$\dfrac{D}{C} = \dfrac{2 \text{ dogs}}{3 \text{ cats}}$, where D and C are variables standing for the number of dogs and cats, respectively.

However, do not just write $\dfrac{x}{y} = \dfrac{2}{3}$. You could easily forget which variable stands for cats and which for

dogs.

Also, NEVER write $\dfrac{2d}{3c}$. The reason is that you might think that d and c stand for *variables*—that

is, numbers in their own right. Always write the full unit out.

Proportions

Simple ratio problems can be solved with a proportion.

> The ratio of girls to boys in the class is 4 to 7. If there are 35 boys in the class, how many girls are there?

Step 1: Set up a labeled PROPORTION:

$$\frac{4 \text{ girls}}{7 \text{ boys}} = \frac{x \text{ girls}}{35 \text{ boys}}$$

Step 2: Cross-multiply to solve:

$$140 = 7x$$
$$x = 20$$

To save time, you should cancel factors out of proportions before cross-multiplying. You can cancel factors either vertically within a fraction or horizontally across an equals sign:

$$\frac{4 \text{ girls}}{7 \text{ boys}} = \frac{x \text{ girls}}{35 \text{ boys}} \qquad \frac{4 \text{ girls}}{\cancel{7} \; 1 \text{ boy}} = \frac{x \text{ girls}}{\cancel{35} \; 5 \text{ boys}} \qquad x = 20$$

Never cancel factors diagonally across an equals sign. That would change the values incorrectly.

Check Your Skills

1. The ratio of apples to oranges in a fruit basket is 3:5. If there are 15 apples, how many oranges are there?

2. Mike has 7 jazz CDs for every 12 classical CDs in his collection. If he has 60 classical CDs, how many jazz CDs does he have?

Answers can be found on page 55.

The Unknown Multiplier

For more complicated ratio problems, the "Unknown Multiplier" technique is useful.

> The ratio of men to women in a room is 3 : 4. If there are 56 people in the room, how many of the people are men?

Using the methods from the previous page, you can write the ratio relationship as $\dfrac{M \text{ men}}{W \text{ women}} = \dfrac{3}{4}$.

Together with $M + W = \text{Total} = 56$, you can solve for M (and W, for that matter). The algebra for these "two equations and two unknowns" is not too difficult.

However, there is even an easier way. It requires a slight shift in your thinking, but if you can make this shift, you can save yourself a lot of work on some problems. Instead of representing the number of men as M, represent it as $3x$, where x is some unknown (positive) number. Likewise, instead of representing the number of women as W, represent it as $4x$, where x is the same unknown number. In this case (as in many others), x has to be a whole number. This is another example of a hidden constraint.

What does this seemingly odd step accomplish? It guarantees that the ratio of men to women is 3 : 4. The ratio of men to women can now be expressed as $\dfrac{3x}{4x}$, which reduces to $\dfrac{3}{4}$, the desired ratio. (Note that we can cancel the x's because we know that x is not zero.) This variable x is known as the Unknown Multiplier. The Unknown Multiplier allows us to reduce the number of variables, making the algebra easier.

Now determine the value of the Unknown Multiplier, using the other equation.

$$\text{Men} + \text{Women} = \text{Total} = 56$$
$$3x + 4x = 56$$
$$7x = 56$$
$$x = 8$$

Now we know that the value of x, the Unknown Multiplier, is 8. Therefore, we can determine the exact number of men and women in the room:

The number of men = $3x = 3(8) = 24$. The number of women = $4x = 4(8) = 32$.

When *can* you use the Unknown Multiplier? You can use it ONCE per problem. Every other ratio in the problem must be set up with a proportion using the already defined unknown multiplier. You should never have two Unknown Multipliers in the same problem.

When *should* you use the Unknown Multiplier? You should use it when neither quantity in the ratio is already equal to a number or a variable expression. Generally, the first ratio in a problem can be set up with an Unknown Multiplier. In the "girls & boys" problem on the previous page, however, we can glance ahead and see that the number of boys is given as 35. This means that we can just set up a simple proportion to solve the problem.

The Unknown Multiplier is particularly useful with three-part ratios:

> A recipe calls for amounts of lemon juice, wine, and water in the ratio of
> $2 : 5 : 7$. If all three combined yield 35 milliliters of liquid, how much wine was included?

Make a quick table: Lemon Juice + Wine + Water = Total
                            $2x$ + $5x$ + $7x$ = $14x$

Now solve: $14x = 35$, or $x = 2.5$. Thus, the amount of wine is $5x = 5(2.5) = 12.5$ milliliters.

In this problem, the Unknown Multiplier turns out not to be an integer. This result is fine, because the problem deals with continuous quantities (milliliters of liquids). In problems like the first one, which deals with integer quantities (men and women), the Unknown Multipier must be a positive integer. In that specific problem, the multiplier is literally the number of "complete sets" of 3 men and 4 women each.

Check Your Skills

3. The ratio of apples to oranges in a fruit basket is 3:5. If there are a total of 48 fruit, how many oranges are there?
4. Steve has nuts, bolts and washers in the ratio 5:4:6. If he has a total of 180 pieces of hardware, how many bolts does he have?
5. A dry mixture consists of 3 cups of flour for every 2 cups of sugar. How much sugar is in 4 cups of the mixture?

Answers can be found on page 55.

Multiple Ratios: Make a Common Term

You may encounter two ratios containing a common element. To combine the ratios, you can use a process remarkably similar to creating a common denominator for fractions.

Because ratios act like fractions, you can multiply both sides of a ratio (or all sides, if there are more than two) by the same number, just as you can multiply the numerator and denominator of a fraction by the same number. You can change *fractions* to have common *denominators*. Likewise, you can change *ratios* to have common *terms* corresponding to the same quantity. Consider the following problem:

> In a box containing action figures of the three Fates from Greek mythology, there are three figures of Clotho for every two figures of Atropos, and five figures of Clotho for every four figures of Lachesis.
> (a)   What is the least number of action figures that could be in the box?
> (b)   What is the ratio of Lachesis figures to Atropos figures?

(a) In symbols, this problem tells you that $C : A = 3 : 2$ and $C : L = 5 : 4$. You cannot instantly combine these ratios into a single ratio of all three quantities, because the terms for C are different. However, you can fix that problem by multiplying each ratio by the right number, making both *C*'s into the *least common multiple* of the current values.

C : A : L		C : A : L
3 : 2	→ Multiply by 5 →	15 : 10
5 : : 4	→ Multiply by 3 →	15 : : 12

This is the combined ratio: $\boxed{15 : 10 : 12}$

The actual *numbers* of action figures are these three numbers times an Unknown Multiplier, which must be a positive integer. Using the smallest possible multiplier, 1, there are $15 + 12 + 10 = 37$ action figures.

(b) Once you have combined the ratios, you can extract the numbers corresponding to the quantities in question and disregard the others: $L : A = 12 : 10$, which reduces to 6 : 5.

Check Your Skills

6. A school has 3 freshmen for every 4 sophomores and 5 sophomores for every 4 juniors. If there are 240 juniors in the school, how many freshmen are there?

Answers can be found on page 56.

Check Your Skills Answers

1. **25:** Set up a proportion:

$$\frac{3 \text{ apples}}{5 \text{ oranges}} = \frac{15 \text{ apples}}{x \text{ oranges}}$$

Now cross multiply:

$3x = 5 \times 15$
$3x = 75$
$x = 25$

2. **35:** Set up a proportion:

$$\frac{7 \text{ jazz}}{12 \text{ classical}} = \frac{x \text{ jazz}}{60 \text{ classical}}$$

Now cross multiply:

$7 \times 60 = 12x$
$420 = 12x$
$35 = x$

3. **30:** Using the unknown multiplier, label the number of apples $3x$ and the number of oranges $5x$. Make a quick table:

Apples	+	Oranges	=	Total
$3x$	+	$5x$	=	$8x$

The total is equal to $8x$, and there are 48 total fruit, so

$8x = 48$
$x = 6$
Oranges $= 5x = 5(6) = 30$

4. **48:** Using the unknown multiplier, label the number of nuts $5x$, the number of bolts $4x$ and the number of washers $6x$. The total is $5x + 4x + 6x$.

$5x + 4x + 6x = 180$
$15x = 180$
$x = 12$

The total number of bolts is $4(12) = 48$

5. **8/5:** Using the unknown multiplier, label the amount of flour $3x$, and the amount of sugar $2x$. The total amount of mixture is $3x + 2x = 5x$.

$5x = 4$ (cups)

$x = 4/5$

The total amount of sugar is $2(4/5) = 8/5$ cups

6. **225:** Use a table to organize the different ratios:

F : S : J

3 : 4   (3 freshmen for every 4 sophomores)

    5 : 4   (5 sophomores for every 4 juniors)

Sophomores appear in both ratios, as 4 in the first and 5 in the second. The lowest common denominator of 4 and 5 is 20. Multiply the ratios accordingly:

F : S : J   F : S : J

3 : 4   →   Multiply by 5 →   15 : 20

    5 : 4   →   Multiply by 4 →   20 : 16

The final ratio is F : S : J = 15 : 20 : 16. There are 240 juniors. Use a ratio to solve for the number of freshmen:

$$\frac{16}{240} = \frac{15}{x}$$

$$\frac{1}{15} = \frac{15}{x}$$

$$x = 225$$

Problem Set

Solve the following problems, using the strategies you have learned in this section. Use proportions and the unknown multiplier to organize ratios.

For problems 1 through 5, assume that neither x nor y is equal to 0, to permit division by x and by y.

1.   48 : 2x is equivalent to 144 : 600. What is x?

2. x : 15 is equivalent to y to x. Given that $y = 3x$, what is x?

3.   Brian's marbles have a red to yellow ratio of 2 : 1. If Brian has 22 red marbles, how many yellow marbles does Brian have?

4.   Initially, the men and women in a room were in the ratio of 5 : 7. Six women leave the room. If there are 35 men in the room, how many women are left in the room?

5.   It is currently raining cats and dogs in the ratio of 5 : 6. If there are 18 fewer cats than dogs, how many dogs are raining?

6.   The amount of time that three people worked on a special project was in the ratio of 2 to 3 to 5. If the project took 110 hours, how many more hours did the hardest working person work than the person who worked the least?

7.

A group of students and teachers take a field trip, such that the student to teacher ratio is 8 to 1. The total number of people on the field trip is between 60 and 70.

Column A

The number of teachers on the field trip

Column B

6

8.

The ratio of men to women on a panel was 3 to 4 before one woman was replaced by a man.

Column A

The number of men on the panel

Column B

The number of women on the panel

9.

A bracelet contains rubies, emer-
alds and sapphires, such that
there are two rubies for every
emerald and five sapphires for
every three rubies.

Column A

The minimum possible number
of gemstones on the bracelet

Column B

20

1. **100:**

$$\frac{48}{2x} = \frac{144}{600}$$ Simplify the ratios and cancel factors horizontally across the equals sign.

$$\frac{\cancel{24}\ 4}{x} = \frac{\cancel{6}\ 1}{25}$$ Then, cross-multiply: $x = 100$.

2. **45:**

$$\frac{x}{15} = \frac{y}{x}$$ First, substitute $3x$ for y.

$$\frac{x}{15} = \frac{3x}{x} = 3$$ Then, solve for x: $x = 3 \times 15 = 45$.

3. **11:** Write a proportion to solve this problem: $$\frac{\text{red}}{\text{yellow}} = \frac{2}{1} = \frac{22}{x}$$

Cross-multiply to solve: $2x = 22$

$x = 11$

4 **43:** First, establish the starting number of men and women with a proportion, and simplify.

$$\frac{5 \text{ men}}{7 \text{ women}} = \frac{35 \text{ men}}{x \text{ women}} \qquad \frac{\cancel{5}\ 1 \text{ man}}{7 \text{ women}} = \frac{\cancel{35}\ 7 \text{ men}}{x \text{ women}}$$

Cross-multiply: $x = 49$.

If 6 women leave the room, there are $49 - 6 = 43$ women left.

5. **108:** If the ratio of cats to dogs is 5 : 6, then there are $5x$ cats and $6x$ dogs (using the Unknown Multiplier). Express the fact that there are 18 fewer cats than dogs with an equation:

$$5x + 18 = 6x$$
$$x = 18$$

Therefore, there are $6(18) = 108$ dogs.

6. **33 hours:** Use an equation with the Unknown Multiplier to represent the total hours put in by the three people:

$$2x + 3x + 5x = 110$$
$$10x = 110$$
$$x = 11$$

Therefore, the hardest working person put in $5(11) = 55$ hours, and the person who worked the least put in $2(11) = 22$ hours. This represents a difference of $55 - 22 = 33$ hours.

7. **A:** We can use an Unknown Multiplier x to help express the number of students and teachers. In light of the given ratio there would be x teachers and $8x$ students, and the total number of people on the field trip would therefore be $x + 8x = 9x$. Note that x in this case must be a positive integer, because we cannot have fractional people.

The total number of people must therefore be a multiple of 9. The only multiple of 9 between 60 and 70 is 63. Therefore x must be $63/9 = 7$. Rewrite the columns:

Column A

The number of teachers on the field

trip = 7

Column B

6

8. **D:** While we know the ratio of men to women, we do not know the actual number of men and women. The following Before and After charts illustrate two of many possibilities:

Case 1	Men	Women
Before	3	4
After	4	3

Case 2	Men	Women
Before	6	8
After	7	7

These charts illustrate that the number of men may or may not be greater than the number of women after the move.

9. **B:** This Multiple Ratio problem is complicated by the fact that the number of rubies is not consistent between the two given ratios, appearing as 2 in one and 3 in the other. We can use the least common multiple of 2 and 3 to make the number of rubies the same in both ratios:

$E : R : S$ $E : R : S$
1 : 2   multiply by 3   3 : 6
   3 : 5   multiply by 2   6 : 10

Combining the two ratios into a single ratio yields

$E : R : S :$ Total = 3 : 6 : 10 : 19

Note that the Total can be obtained as the sum of all preceding parts in the ratio. The total number of gemstones must therefore be a positive integer multiple of 19, of which the smallest is 19 itself. Rewrite the columns:

Column A

The minimum possible number
of gemstones on the bracelet = 19

Column B

20

Chapter 4
of
WORD TRANSLATIONS

STATISTICS

In This Chapter . . .

AVERAGES

The **average** (or the **arithmetic mean**) of a set is given by the following formula (also known as "the average formula"):

$$\text{Average} = \frac{\text{Sum}}{\text{\# of terms}}, \text{ which is abbreviated as } A = \frac{S}{n}.$$

The sum, S, refers to the sum of all the terms in the set.
The number, n, refers to the number of terms that are in the set.
The average, A, refers to the average value (arithmetic mean) of the terms in the set.

The language in an average problem will often refer to an "arithmetic mean." However, occasionally the concept is implied. "The cost per employee, if equally shared, is $20" means that the <u>average</u> cost per employee is $20.

A commonly used variation of the Average formula is:

$$(\text{Average}) \times (\text{\# of terms}) = (\text{Sum}), \text{ or } A \cdot n = S.$$

This formula has the same basic form as the $RT = D$ equation, so it lends itself readily to the same kind of table you would use for RTD problems.

Every GRE problem dealing with averages can be solved with the average formula. If you are asked to use or find the average of a set, you should not concentrate on the individual terms of the set. As you can see from the formulas above, all that matters is the *sum* of the terms—which can often be found even if the individual terms cannot be determined.

Using the Average Formula

The first thing to do for any GRE average problem is to write down the average formula. Then, fill in any of the 3 variables (S, n, and A) that are given in the problem.

> The sum of 6 numbers is 90. What is the average term?

$$A = \frac{S}{n}$$

Notice that you do NOT need to know each term in the set to find the average!

The sum, S, is given as 90. The number of terms, n, is given as 6.

By plugging in, we can solve for the average: $\frac{90}{6} = 15$.

Sometimes, using the average formula will be more involved. For example:

> If the average of the set {2, 5, 5, 7, 8, 9, x} is 6.1, what is the value of x?

Plug the given information into the average formula, and solve for x.

$$A \cdot n = S$$

$$(6.1)(7 \text{ terms}) = 2 + 5 + 5 + 7 + 8 + 9 + x$$
$$42.7 = 36 + x$$
$$6.7 = x$$

More complex average problems involve setting up two average formulas. For example:

> Sam earned a $2,000 commission on a big sale, raising his average commission by $100. If Sam's new average commission is $900, how many sales has he made?

To keep track of two average formulas in the same problem, you can set up an *RTD*-style table. Instead of $RT = D$, we use $A \cdot n = S$, which has the same form.

Note that the Number and Sum columns add up to give the new cumulative values, but the values in the Average column do *not* add up:

	Average	×	Number	=	Sum
Old Total	800	×	n	=	$800n$
This Sale	2000	×	1	=	2000
New Total	900	×	$n + 1$	=	$900(n + 1)$

The right-hand column gives the equation we need:
$$800n + 2000 = 900(n + 1)$$
$$800n + 2000 = 900n + 900$$
$$1100 = 100n$$
$$11 = n$$

Since we are looking for the new number of sales, which is $n + 1$, Sam has made a total of 12 sales.

Check Your Skills

1. The sum of 6 integers is 45. What is the average of the six integers?
2. The average price per item in a shopping basket is $2.40. If there are a total of 30 items in the basket, what is the total price of the items in the basket?

Answers can be found on page 69.

Evenly Spaced Sets: Take the Middle

You may recall that the average of a set of consecutive integers is the middle number (the middle number of <u>any</u> set is always its median – more on this later). This is true for any set in which the terms are spaced evenly apart. For example:

The average of the set {3, 5, 7, 9, 11} is the middle term 7, because all the terms in the set are spaced evenly apart (in this case, they are spaced 2 units apart).

The average of the set {12, 20, 28, 36, 44, 52, 60, 68, 76} is the middle term 44, because all the terms in the set are spaced evenly apart (in this case, they are spaced 8 units apart).

Note that if an evenly spaced set has two "middle" numbers, the average of the set is the average of these two middle numbers. For example:

The average of the set {5, 10, 15, 20, 25, 30} is 17.5, because this is the average of the two middle numbers, 15 and 20.

You do not have to write out each term of an evenly spaced set to find the middle number—the average term. All you need to do to find the middle number is to add the **first** and **last** terms and divide that sum by 2. For example:

The average of the set {101, 111, 121...581, 591, 601} is equal to 351, which is the sum of the first and last terms (101 + 601 = 702) divided by 2. This approach is especially attractive if the number of terms is large.

Check Your Skills

3. What is the average of the set {2, 5, 8, 11, 14}?
4. What is the average of the set {−1, 3, 7, 11, 15, 19, 23, 27}?

Answers can be found on page 69.

Weighted Averages

Properties of Weighted Averages

Although weighted averages differ from traditional averages, they are still averages—meaning that their values will still fall *between* the values being averaged (or between the highest and lowest of those values, if there are more than two).

A weighted average of only *two* values will fall closer to whichever value is weighted more heavily. For instance, if a drink is made by mixing 2 shots of a liquor containing 15% alcohol with 3 shots of a liquor containing 20% alcohol, then the alcohol content of the mixed drink will be closer to 20% than to 15%.

Here's another example, take the weighted average of 20 and 30, with weights $\dfrac{a}{a+b}$ and $\dfrac{b}{a+b}$.

$$\text{Weighted average} = \dfrac{a}{a+b}(20) + \dfrac{b}{a+b}(30)$$

The weighted average will always be between 20 and 30, as long as a and b are both positive (and on the GRE, they always have been). A number line between 20 and 30 displays where the weighted average will fall:

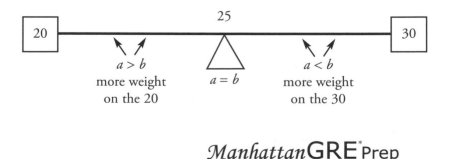

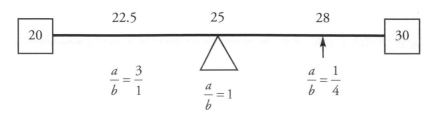

Check Your Skills

5. A stock portfolio is comprised of Stock A, whose annual gain was 10%, and Stock B, whose annual gain was 20%. If the stock portfolio gained 14% overall, does it contain more shares of Stock A or Stock B?

6. 2/3 of the aliens on Planet X are Zorgs, whose average IQ is 120. The rest are Weebs, whose average IQ is 180. What is the average IQ of all the aliens on Planet X?

Answers can be found on page 69.

Median: The Middle Number

Some GRE problems feature a second type of average: the *median*, or "middle value." The median is calculated in one of two ways, depending on the number of data points in the set.

For sets containing an **odd** number of values, the median is the **unique middle value** when the data are arranged in increasing (or decreasing) order.

For sets containing an **even** number of values, the median is the **average (arithmetic mean) of the two middle values** when the data are arranged in increasing (or decreasing) order.

The median of the set {5, 17, 24, 25, 28} is the unique middle number, 24. The median of the set {3, 4, 9, 9} is the mean of the two middle values (4 and 9), or 6.5. Notice that the median of a set containing an *odd* number of values must be a value in the set. However, the median of a set containing an *even* number of values does not have to be in the set—and indeed will not be, unless the two middle values are equal.

Medians of Sets Containing Unknown Values

Unlike the arithmetic mean, the median of a set depends only on the one or two values in the middle of the ordered set. Therefore, you may be able to determine a specific value for the median of a set *even if one or more unknowns are present.*

For instance, consider the unordered set {x, 2, 5, 11, 11, 12, 33}. No matter whether x is less than 11, equal to 11, or greater than 11, the median of the resulting set will be 11. (Try substituting different values of x to see why the median does not change.)

By contrast, the median of the unordered set {x, 2, 5, 11, 12, 12, 33} depends on x. If x is 11 or less, the median is 11. If x is between 11 and 12, the median is x. Finally, if x is 12 or more, the median is 12.

Check Your Skills

7. What is the median of the set {6, 2, −1, 4, 0}?

8. What is the median of the set {1, 2, 4, 8}?

Answers can be found on page 69.

Standard Deviation

The mean and median both give "average" or "representative" values for a set, but they do not tell the whole story. It is possible for two sets to have the same average but to differ widely in how spread out their values are. To describe the spread, or variation, of the data in a set, we use a different measure: the Standard Deviation.

Standard Deviation (SD) indicates how far from the average (mean) the data points typically fall. Therefore:

A small SD indicates that a set is clustered closely around the average (mean) value.

A large SD indicates that the set is spread out widely, with some points appearing far from the mean.

Consider the sets {5, 5, 5, 5}, {2, 4, 6, 8}, and {0, 0, 10, 10}. These sets all have the same mean value of 5. You can see at a glance, though, that the sets are very different, and the differences are reflected in their SDs. The first set has a SD of zero (no spread at all), the second set has a moderate SD, and the third set has a large SD.

The formula for calculating SD is rather cumbersome. The good news is that you do not need to know—**it is very unlikely that a GRE problem will ask you to calculate an exact SD**. If you just pay attention to what the *average spread* is doing, you'll be able to answer all GRE standard deviation problems, which involve either (a) *changes* in the SD when a set is transformed or (b) *comparisons* of the SDs of two or more sets. Just remember that the more spread out the numbers, the larger the SD.

If you see a problem focusing on changes in the SD, ask yourself whether the changes move the data closer to the mean, farther from the mean, or neither. If you see a problem requiring comparisons, ask yourself which set is more spread out from its mean.

You should also know the term "variance," which is just the square of the standard deviation.

Following are some sample problems to help illustrate standard deviation properties:

(a) Which set has the greater standard deviation: {1, 2, 3, 4, 5} or {440, 442, 443, 444, 445}?
(b) If each data point in a set is increased by 7, does the set's standard deviation increase, decrease, or remain constant?
(c) If each data point in a set is increased by a factor of 7, does the set's standard deviation increase, decrease, or remain constant?

(a) The second set has the greater SD. One way to understand this is to observe that the gaps between its numbers are, on average, slightly bigger than the gaps in the first set (because the first 2 numbers are 2 units apart). Another way to resolve the issue is to observe that the set {441, 442, 443, 444, 445} would have the same standard deviation as {1, 2, 3, 4, 5}. Replacing 441 with 440, which is farther from the mean, will increase the SD.

In any case, only the *spread* matters. The numbers in the second set are much more "consistent" in some sense—they are all within about 1% of each other, while the largest numbers in the first set are several times the smallest ones. However, this "percent variation" idea is irrelevant to the SD.

(b) The SD will not change. "Increased by 7" means that the number 7 is *added* to each data point in the set. This transformation will not affect any of the gaps between the data points, and thus it will not affect how far the data points are from the mean. If the set were plotted on a number line, this transformation would merely slide the points 7 units to the right, taking all the gaps, and the mean, along with them.

(c) The SD will increase. "Increased by a *factor* of 7" means that each data point is multiplied by 7. This transformation will make all the gaps between points 7 times as big as they originally were. Thus, each point will fall 7 times as far from the mean. The SD will increase by a factor of 7.

Check Your Skills

9. Which set has a greater standard deviation?

Set A: {3, 4, 5, 6, 7}   Set B: {3, 3, 5, 7, 7}

Answers can be found on page 69–70.

Check Your Skills Answers

1. **7.5:** $A = \dfrac{S}{n}$

$A = \dfrac{45}{6} = 7.5$

2. **$72:** $A = \dfrac{S}{n}$

$2.40 = \dfrac{S}{30}$

$S = 2.40(30) = 72$

3. **8:** Notice that each term in the set is 3 more than the last. Because this set is evenly spaced, the median and the average will be the same. The median is 8, and so the average is also 8.

4. **13:** Notice that each term in the set is 4 more than the last. Because this set is evenly spaced, the median and the average will be the same. The number of terms in the set is even, so the median of the set is the average of the two middle terms: $A = (11 + 15)/2 = 13$

5. **Stock A:** Because the overall gain is closer to 10% than to 20%, the portfolio must be weighted more heavily towards Stock A, i.e., contain more shares of Stock A.

6. **140:** 2/3 of the total population is Zorgs, and so the weight is 2/3. Similarly, the weight of the Weebs is 1/3. Now plug everything into the weighted average formula:

$$\text{Weighted Average} = \frac{2}{3}(120) + \frac{1}{3}(120)$$
$$= 80 + 60$$
$$= 140$$

7. **2:** First order the set from least to greatest:

$$\{6, 2, -1, 4, 0\} \rightarrow \{-1, 0, 2, 4, 6\}$$

The median is the middle number, which is 2.

8. **3:** Because the number of terms is even, the median is the average of the two middle terms: $\dfrac{2+4}{2} = 3$.

9. **Set B:** Each set has a mean of 5, so the set whose numbers are further away from the mean will have the higher standard deviation. When comparing standard deviations, focus on the differences between each set. The numbers that each set has in common are highlighted:

Set A: {**3**, 4, **5**, 6, **7**}   Set B: {**3**, 3, **5**, 7, 7}

Compare the numbers that are not the same. 4 and 6 in Set A are closer to the mean (5) than are 3 and 7 in Set B. Therefore, the numbers in Set B are further away from the mean and Set B has a larger standard deviation.

Problem Set

1.   The average of 11 numbers is 10. When one number is eliminated, the average of the remaining numbers is 9.3. What is the eliminated number?

2.   The average of 9, 11, and 16 is equal to the average of 21, 4.6, and what number?

3.   Given the set of numbers {4, 5, 5, 6, 7, 8, 21}, how much higher is the mean than the median?

4.   The sum of 8 numbers is 168. If one of the numbers is 28, what is the average of the other 7 numbers?

5.   If the average of the set {5, 6, 6, 8, 9, x, y} is 6, then what is the value of $x + y$?

6.   On 4 sales, Matt received commissions of $300, $40, $$x$, and $140. Without the $$x$, his average commission would be $50 lower. What is x?

7.   The class mean score on a test was 60, and the standard deviation was 15. If Elena's score was within 2 standard deviations of the mean, what is the lowest score she could have received?

8.   Matt gets a $1,000 commission on a big sale. This commission alone raises his average commission by $150. If Matt's new average commission is $400, how many sales has Matt made?

9.   Grace's average bowling score over the past 6 games is 150. If she wants to raise her average score by 10%, and she has two games left in the season, what must her average score on the last two games be?

10.   If the average of x and y is 50, and the average of y and z is 80, what is the value of $z - x$?

11.

A college class is attended by Poets and Bards in the ratio of three Poets for every two Bards. On a midterm the average score of the Poets is 60 and the average score of the Bards is 80.

Column A

The overall average score for the class

Column B

70

12.

$$x > 2$$

Column A

The median of $x - 4$, $x + 1$, and $4x$

Column B

The mean of $x - 4$, $x + 1$, and $4x$

13.

A is the set of the first five positive odd integers. B is the set of the first five positive even integers.

Column A

The standard deviation of A

Column B

The standard deviation of B

1. **17:** If the average of 11 numbers is 10, their sum is $11 \times 10 = 110$. After one number is eliminated, the average is 9.3, so the sum of the 10 remaining numbers is $10 \times 9.3 = 93$. The number eliminated is the difference between these sums: $110 - 93 = 17$.

2. **10.4:** $\dfrac{9+11+16}{3} = \dfrac{21+4.6+x}{3}$ $9 + 11 + 16 = 21 + 4.6 + x$ $x = 10.4$

3. **2:** The mean of the set is the sum of the numbers divided by the number of terms: $56 \div 7 = 8$. The median is the middle number: 6. 8 is 2 greater than 6.

4. **20:** The sum of the other 7 numbers is 140 $(168 - 28)$. So, the average of the numbers is $140/7 = 20$.

5. **8:** If the average of 7 terms is 6, then the sum of the terms is 7×6, or 42. The listed terms have a sum of 34. Therefore, the remaining terms, x and y, must have a sum of $42 - 34$, or 8.

6. **$360:** Without x, Matt's average sale is $(300 + 40 + 140) \div 3$, or $160. With x, Matt's average is $50 more, or $210. Therefore, the sum of $(300 + 40 + 140 + x) = 4(210) = 840$, and $x = 360.

7. **30:** Elena's score was within 2 standard deviations of the mean. Since the standard deviation is 15, her score is no more than 30 points from the mean. The lowest possible score she could have received, then, is $60 - 30$, or 30.

8. **5:** Before the $1,000 commission, Matt's average commission was $250; we can express this algebraically with the equation $S = 250n$.

After the sale, the sum of Matt's sales increased by $1,000, the number of sales made increased by 1, and his average commission was $400. We can express this algebraically with the equation:

$$S + 1,000 = 400(n + 1)$$

$$250n + 1,000 = 400(n + 1)$$
$$250n + 1,000 = 400n + 400$$
$$150n = 600$$
$$n = 4$$

Before the big sale, Matt had made 4 sales. Including the big sale, Matt has made 5 sales.

9. **210:** Grace wants to raise her average score by 10%. Since 10% of 150 is 15, her target average is 165. Grace's total score is 150×6, or 900. If, in 8 games, she wants to have an average score of 165, then she will need a total score of 165×8, or 1,320. This is a difference of $1,320 - 900$, or 420. Her average score in the next two games must be: $420 \div 2 = 210$.

10. **60:** The sum of two numbers is twice their average. Therefore,

$$x + y = 100 \qquad\qquad y + z = 160$$
$$x = 100 - y \qquad\qquad z = 160 - y$$

Substitute these expressions for z and x:

$$z - x = (160 - y) - (100 - y) = 160 - y - 100 + y = 160 - 100 = 60$$

*Manhattan*GRE*Prep

Alternatively, pick Smart Numbers for x and y. Let $x = 50$ and $y = 50$ (this is an easy way to make their average equal 50). Since the average of y and z must be 80, we have $z = 110$. Therefore, $z - x = 110 - 50 = 60$.

11. **B:** This is a Weighted Average problem. The overall average score can be computed by assigning weights to the average scores of Poets and Bards that reflect the number of people in each subgroup. Because the ratio of Poets to Bards is 3 to 2, and collectively the two groups account for all students, the multiple ratio may be written as $P : B : Total = 3 : 2 : 5$.

This means that Poets constitute 3/5 of the students and Bards the remaining 2/5. Therefore, the overall average score is given by the weighted average formula:

$$\frac{3}{5} \times 60 + \frac{2}{5} \times 80 = 68$$

Alternatively, we may argue as follows: if there were the same number of Poets as there were Bards, the overall average score would be 70. However, there are actually more Poets than Bards, so the overall average score will be closer to 60 than to 80, i.e., less than 70.

12. **B:** Let us begin with the median. In a set with an odd number of terms, the median will be the middle term when the terms are put in ascending order. It is clear that $x + 1 > x - 4$. Moreover, because $x > 2$, $4x$ must be greater than $x + 1$. Therefore the median is $x + 1$. Rewrite Column A:

$$x > 2$$

Column A	**Column B**
The median of $x - 4$, $x + 1$, and $4x = x + 1$	The mean of $x - 4$, $x + 1$, and $4x$

In order to compute the mean, we add all three terms and divide by 3:

$$\text{Mean} = \frac{(x-4)+(x+1)+4x}{3} = \frac{6x-3}{3} = 2x-1$$

Rewrite Column B:

$$x > 2$$

Column A	**Column B**
The median of $x - 4$, $x + 1$, and $4x = \boldsymbol{x + 1}$	The mean of $x - 4$, $x + 1$, and $4x = \boldsymbol{2x - 1}$

The comparison thus boils down to which is larger, $x + 1$ or $2x - 1$. The answer is not immediately clear. Subtract x from both sides to try and isolate x.

*Manhattan*GRE Prep
the new standard

$$x > 2$$

Column A	**Column B**
$x + 1$	$2x - 1$
$\underline{-x}$	$\underline{-x}$
1	$x - 1$

Now add one to both sides to isolate x

$$x > 2$$

Column A	**Column B**
$1 + 1 = \mathbf{2}$	$(x - 1) + 1 = \boldsymbol{x}$

The common information states that x must be larger than 2, so Column B must be larger.

13. **C:** The sets in question are $A = \{1, 3, 5, 7, 9\}$ and $B = \{2, 4, 6, 8, 10\}$. Each is a set of evenly spaced integers with an odd number of terms, such that the mean is the middle number. The deviations between the elements of the set and the mean of the set in each case are the same: -4, -2, 0, 2 and 4. Thus the standard deviations of the sets must also be the same.

Chapter 5
of
WORD TRANSLATIONS

COMBINATORICS

In This Chapter . . .

- The Fundamental Counting Principle
- Simple Factorials
- Anagrams
- Combinatorics with Repetition: Anagram Grids
- Multiple Arrangements

COMBINATORICS

Many GRE problems are, ultimately, just about counting things. Although counting may seem to be a simple concept, counting *problems* can be complex. In fact, counting problems have given rise to a whole subfield of mathematics: *combinatorics*, which is essentially "advanced counting." This chapter presents the fundamentals of combinatorics that are essential on the GRE.

In combinatorics, we are often counting the **number of possibilities**: how many different ways you can arrange things. For instance, we might ask the following:

(1)   A restaurant menu features five appetizers, six entrées, and three desserts. If a dinner special consists of one appetizer, one entrée, and one dessert, how many different dinner specials are possible?
(2)   Four people sit down in 4 fixed chairs lined up in a row. How many different seating arrangements are possible?
(3)   If there are 7 people in a room, but only 3 chairs in a row, how many different seating arrangements are possible?
(4)   If a group of 3 people is to be chosen from 7 people in a room, how many different groups are possible?

The Fundamental Counting Principle

Counting problems commonly feature multiple separate choices. Whether such choices are made simultaneously (e.g., choosing types of bread and filling for a sandwich) or sequentially (e.g., choosing among routes between successive towns on a road trip), the rule for combining the numbers of options is the same.

Fundamental Counting Principle: If you must make a number of separate decisions, then MULTIPLY the numbers of ways to make each *individual* decision to find the number of ways to make *all* the decisions.

To grasp this principle intuitively, imagine that you are making a simple sandwich. You will choose ONE type of bread out of 2 types (Rye or Whole wheat) and ONE type of filling out of 3 types (Chicken salad, Peanut butter, or Tuna fish). How many different kinds of sandwich can you make? Well, you can always list all the possibilities:

Rye – Chicken salad	Whole wheat – Chicken salad
Rye – Peanut butter	Whole wheat – Peanut butter
Rye – Tuna fish	Whole wheat – Tuna fish

We see that there are 6 possible sandwiches overall in this table. Instead of listing all the sandwiches, you can simply **multiply** the number of bread choices by the number of filling choices, as dictated by the Fundamental Counting Principle:

$$2 \text{ breads} \times 3 \text{ fillings} = 6 \text{ possible sandwiches.}$$

As its name implies, the Fundamental Counting Principle is essential to solving combinatorics problems. It is the basis of many other techniques that appear later in this chapter. You can also use the Fundamental Counting Principle directly.

A restaurant menu features five appetizers, six entrées, and three desserts. If a dinner special consists of one appetizer, one entrée, and one dessert, how many different dinner specials are possible?

This problem features three decisions: an appetizer (which can be chosen in 5 different ways), an entrée (6 ways), and a dessert (3 ways). Since the choices are separate, the total number of dinner specials is the product $5 \times 6 \times 3 = 90$.

In theory, you could *list* all 90 dinner specials. In practice, that is the last thing you would ever want to do! It would take far too long, and it is likely that you would make a mistake. Multiplying is much easier—and more accurate.

Check Your Skills

1. How many ways are there of getting from Alphaville to Gammerburg via Betancourt, if there are three roads between Alphaville and Betancourt and four roads between Betancourt and Gammerburg?
2. John can choose between blue, black and brown pants, white, yellow or pink shirts, and whether or not he wears a tie to go with his shirt. How many days can John go without wearing the same combination twice?

Answers can be found on page 85.

Simple Factorials

You are often asked to count the possible arrangements of a set of distinct objects (e.g., "Four people sit down in 4 fixed chairs lined up in a row. How many different seating arrangements are possible?") To count these arrangements, use *factorials*:

The number of ways of putting *n* distinct objects in order, if there are no restrictions, is *n*! (*n* factorial).

The term "*n* factorial" (*n*!) refers to the product of all the positive integers from 1 through *n*, inclusive: $n! = (n)(n-1)(n-2)...(3)(2)(1)$. You should learn the factorials through 6!:

$1! = 1$	$4! = 4 \times 3 \times 2 \times 1 = 24$
$2! = 2 \times 1 = 2$	$5! = 5 \times 4 \times 3 \times 2 \times 1 = 120$
$3! = 3 \times 2 \times 1 = 6$	$6! = 6 \times 5 \times 4 \times 3 \times 2 \times 1 = 720$

n! counts the rearrangements of *n* distinct objects as a special (but very common) application of the Slot Method. For example consider the case of *n* = 4, with 4 people and 4 fixed chairs. Let each slot represent a chair. Place any one of the 4 people in the first chair. You now have only 3 choices for the person in the second chair. Next, you have 2 choices for the third chair. Finally, you must put the last person in the last chair: you only have 1 choice. Now multiply together all those separate choices.

Arrangements of 4 people in 4 fixed chairs: $\underline{4} \times \underline{3} \times \underline{2} \times \underline{1} = 4! = 24$

Incidentally, you can certainly use the Slot Method the first few times to ensure that you grasp this formula, but then you should graduate to using the formula directly.

In staging a house, a real-estate agent must place six different books on a bookshelf. In how many different orders can she arrange the books?

Using the Fundamental Counting Principle, we see that we have 6 choices for the book that goes first, 5 choices for the book that goes next, and so forth. Ultimately, we have this total:

$$6! = 6 \times 5 \times 4 \times 3 \times 2 \times 1 = 720 \text{ different orders.}$$

Check Your Skills

3. In how many different ways can the five Olympic rings be colored Black, Red, Green, Yellow and Blue, without changing the arrangement of the rings themselves?
Answers can be found on page 85.

Anagrams

An *anagram* is a rearrangement of the letters in a word or phrase. (Puzzle enthusiasts require the rearrangement itself to be a meaningful word or phrase, but we are also going to include rearrangements that are total nonsense.) For instance, the word DEDUCTIONS is an anagram of DISCOUNTED, and so is the gibberish "word" CDDEINOSTU.

Now that you know about factorials, you can easily count the anagrams of a simple word with *n* distinct letters: simply compute *n*! (*n* factorial).

How many different anagrams (meaningful or nonsense) are possible for the word GRE?

Since there are 3 distinct letters in the word GRE, there are 3! = 6 anagrams of the word.

Check Your Skills

4. In how many different ways can the letters of the word DEPOSIT be arranged (meaningful or nonsense)?
Answers can be found on page 85.

Combinatorics with Repetition: Anagram Grids

Anagrams themselves are unlikely to appear on the GRE. However, many combinatorics problems are exact analogues of anagram problems and can therefore be solved with the same methods developed for the preceding problem. *Most problems involving rearranging objects can be solved by anagramming.*

If seven people board an airport shuttle with only three available seats, how many different seating arrangements are possible? (Assume that three of the seven will actually take the seats.)

Three of the people will take the seats (designated 1, 2, and 3), and the other four will be left standing (designated "S"). The problem is therefore equivalent to finding anagrams of the "word" *123SSSS*, where the four S's are equivalent and indistinguishable. You can construct an **Anagram Grid** to help you make the connection:

Person	A	B	C	D	E	F	G
Seat	1	2	3	S	S	S	S

The top row corresponds to the 7 unique people. The bottom row corresponds to the "seating labels" that we put on those people. Note that some of these labels are repeated (the four S's). In general, you should set up an Anagram Grid to put the unique items or people on top. Only the bottom row should contain any repeated labels.

In this grid, you are free to rearrange the elements in the bottom row (the three seat numbers and the four S's), making "anagrams" that represent all the possible seating arrangements. The number of arrangements is therefore

$$\frac{7!}{4!} = \frac{7 \times 6 \times 5 \times 4 \times 3 \times 2 \times 1}{4 \times 3 \times 2 \times 1} = 7 \times 6 \times 5 = 210$$

Now consider this problem.

> If three of seven standby passengers are selected for a flight, how many different combinations of standby passengers can be selected?

At first, this problem may seem identical to the previous one, because it also involves selecting 3 elements out of a set of 7. However, there is a crucial difference. This time, the three "chosen ones" are *also* indistinguishable, whereas in the earlier problem, the three seats on the shuttle were considered different. As a result, you designate all three flying passengers as *F*'s. The four non-flying passengers are still designated as *N*'s. The problem is then equivalent to finding anagrams of the "word" *FFFNNNN*. Again, you can use an Anagram Grid:

Person	A	B	C	D	E	F	G
Seat	F	F	F	N	N	N	N

To calculate the number of possibilities, we follow the same rule—factorial of the total, divided by the factorials of the repeated letters on the bottom. But notice that this grid is different from the previous one, in which we had *123NNNN* in the bottom row. Here, we divide by *two* factorials, 3! for the *F*'s and 4! for the *N*'s, yielding a much smaller number:

$$\frac{7!}{3! \times 4!} = \frac{7 \times 6 \times 5 \times 4 \times 3 \times 2 \times 1}{(3 \times 2 \times 1) \times (4 \times 3 \times 2 \times 1)} = 7 \times 5 = 35$$

Check Your Skills

5. Peggy will choose 5 of her 8 friends to join her for intramural volleyball. In how many ways can she do so?

Answers can be found on page 85.

Multiple Arrangements

So far, our discussion of combinatorics has revolved around two major topics: (1) the Fundamental Counting Principle and its implications for successive choices, and (2) the anagram approach. The GRE will often *combine* these two ideas on more difficult combinatorics problems, requiring you to choose successive or **multiple arrangements**.

If a GRE problem requires you to choose two or more sets of items from separate pools, count the arrangements <u>separately</u>—perhaps using a different anagram grid each time. Then multiply the numbers of possibilities for each step.

Distinguish these problems—which require choices from *separate pools*—from complex problems that are still single arrangements (all items chosen from the *same pool*). For instance, a problem requiring the choice of a treasurer, a secretary, and three more representatives from <u>one</u> class of 20 students may seem like two or more separate problems, but it is just one: an anagram of one *T*, one *S*, three *R*'s, and fifteen *N*'s in one 20-letter "word."

> The I Eta Pi fraternity must choose a delegation of three senior members and two junior members for an annual interfraternity conference. If I Eta Pi has 12 senior members and 11 junior members, how many different delegations are possible?

This problem involves two genuinely different arrangements: three seniors chosen from a pool of 12 seniors, and two juniors chosen from a *separate* pool of 11 juniors. These arrangements should be calculated separately.

Because the three spots in the delegation are not distinguishable, choosing the seniors is equivalent to choosing an anagram of three *Y*'s and nine *N*'s, which can be accomplished in $\frac{12!}{9! \times 3!} = 220$ different ways. Similarly, choosing the juniors is equivalent to choosing an anagram of two *Y*'s and nine *N*'s, which can be done in $\frac{11!}{9! \times 2!} = 55$ different ways.

Since the choices are successive and independent, multiply the numbers: $220 \times 55 = 12,100$ different delegations are possible.

Check Your Skills

6. Three men (out of 7) and three women (out of 6) will be chosen to serve on a committee. In how many ways can the committee be formed?

Answers can be found on page 85.

Check Your Skills Answers

1. **12:** Multiply the number of choices for each leg of the trip: $3 \times 4 = 12$.

2. **18:** John has 3 choices of pants, 3 choices of shirts and 2 choices involving a tie (yes or no). His total number of choices is $3 \times 2 \times 2 = 18$.

3. **120:** This question is asking for the number of ways to order 5 colored rings with no restrictions.

   $5! = 120$

4. **5,040:** A 7-letter word with all distinct letters has $7! = 5,040$ anagrams.

5. **56:** Produce an Anagram Grid using 1 through 8 for the friends, Y for Yes (i.e., joining Peggy), and N for No (not joining Peggy):

Friend	1	2	3	4	5	6	7	8
Status	Y	Y	Y	Y	Y	N	N	N

Anagram the "word" YYYYYNNN: $\dfrac{8!}{5!\,3!} = \dfrac{8 \times 7 \times 6 \times 5 \times 4 \times 3 \times 2 \times 1}{(5 \times 4 \times 3 \times 2 \times 1) \times (3 \times 2 \times 1)} = \dfrac{8 \times 7 \times 6}{3 \times 2 \times 1} = 56$

6. **700:** For the men, anagram the word YYYNNNN: $\dfrac{7!}{3!\,4!} = \dfrac{7 \times 6 \times 5 \times 4 \times 3 \times 2 \times 1}{(3 \times 2 \times 1) \times (4 \times 3 \times 2 \times 1)} = \dfrac{7 \times 6 \times 5}{3 \times 2 \times 1} = 35$

   For the women, anagram the word YYYNNN: $\dfrac{6!}{3!\,3!} = \dfrac{6 \times 5 \times 4 \times 3 \times 2 \times 1}{(3 \times 2 \times 1) \times (3 \times 2 \times 1)} = \dfrac{6 \times 5 \times 4}{3 \times 2 \times 1} = 20$

Multiply the choices to get the total: $35 \times 20 = 700$ ways. (This is considerably fewer than the number of ways to choose 6 out of 13 people without regard to gender.

Problem Set

Solve the following problems, using the strategies you have learned in this section.

1. In how many different ways can the letters in the word "LEVEL" be arranged?

2. Amy and Adam are making boxes of truffles to give out as wedding favors. They have an unlimited supply of 5 different types of truffles. If each box holds 2 truffles of different types, how many different boxes can they make?

3. A men's basketball league assigns every player a two-digit number for the back of his jersey. If the league uses only the digits 1–5, what is the maximum number of players that can join the league such that no player has a number with a repeated digit (e.g. 22), and no two players have the same number?

4. A pod of 6 dolphins always swims single file, with 3 females at the front and 3 males in the rear. In how many different arrangements can the dolphins swim?

5. A delegation from Gotham City goes to Metropolis to discuss a limited Batman–Superman partnership. If the mayor of Metropolis chooses 3 members of the 7-person delegation to meet with Superman, how many different 3-person combinations can he choose?

6. Mario's Pizza has two choices of crust: deep dish and thin-and-crispy. The restaurant also has a choice of 5 toppings: tomatoes, sausage, peppers, onions, and pepperoni. Finally, Mario's offers every pizza in extra-cheese as well as regular. If Linda's volleyball team decides to order a pizza with four toppings, how many different choices do the teammates have at Mario's Pizza?

7.

Country X has a four-digit postal code assigned to each town, such that the first digit is non-zero, and none of the digits is repeated.

Column A	**Column B**
The number of possible postal codes in Country X	4,500

8.

8 athletes compete in a race in which a gold, a silver and a bronze medal will be awarded to the top three finishers, in that order.

Column A	**Column B**
The number of ways the medals can be awarded	$8 \times 3!$

9.

Lothar has 6 stamps from Utopia and 4 stamps from Cornucopia in his collection. He will give two stamps of each type to his friend Peggy Sue.

<u>**Column A**</u>

The number of ways Lothar can give four stamps (two of each type) to Peggy Sue

<u>**Column B**</u>

100

1. **30:** There are two repeated E's and two repeated L's in the word "LEVEL." To find the anagrams for this word, set up a fraction in which the numerator is the factorial of the number of letters and the denominator is the factorial of the number of each repeated letter.

$$\frac{5!}{2!2!} = \frac{5 \times 4 \times 3 \times 2 \times 1}{2 \times 1 \times 2 \times 1} = 30$$

Alternatively, you can solve this problem using the Slot Method, as long as you correct for over-counting (since you have some indistinguishable elements). There are five choices for the first letter, four for the second, and so on, making the product $5 \times 4 \times 3 \times 2 \times 1 = 120$. However, there are two sets of 2 indistinguishable elements each, so you must divide by 2! to account for each of these. Thus, the total number of combinations is $\dfrac{5 \times 4 \times 3 \times 2 \times 1}{2! \times 2!} = 30$.

2. **10:** In every combination, two types of truffles will be in the box, and three types of truffles will not. Therefore, this problem is a question about the number of anagrams that can be made from the "word" YYNNN:

$$\frac{5!}{2!3!} = \frac{5 \times 4 \times 3 \times 2 \times 1}{3 \times 2 \times 1 \times 2 \times 1} = 5 \times 2 = 10$$

A	B	C	D	E
Y	Y	N	N	N

This problem can also be solved with the formula for combinations, since it is a combination of two items chosen from a set of five (in which order does not matter). Therefore, there are $\dfrac{5!}{2! \times 3!} = 10$ possible combinations.

3. **20:** In this problem, the order of the numbers matters. Each number can be either the tens digit, the units digit, or not a digit in the number. Therefore, this problem is a question about the number of anagrams that can be made from the "word" TUNNN:

$$\frac{5!}{3!} = \frac{5 \times 4 \times 3 \times 2 \times 1}{3 \times 2 \times 1} = 5 \times 4 = 20$$

1	2	3	4	5
T	U	N	N	N

This problem can also be solved with the formula for permutations. The situation is a permutation of two items chosen from a set of five (order matters this time, since switching the two digits produces a genuinely different jersey number).

Therefore, there are $\dfrac{5!}{(5-2)!} = \dfrac{5!}{3!} = 20$ possible permutations. (Remember, in the permutation formula, you always divide, not by the factorial of the number chosen, but by the factorial of the number NOT chosen.)

You can also use the slot method. The slots correspond to the positions of the digits (tens and units). You have 5 choices for the tens digit and then only 4 choices for the units digit (since you cannot use the same digit again), resulting in $5 \times 4 = 20$ possibilities. This method works well for problems in which order matters.

Finally, you can just list out the jersey numbers, since the number of possibilities is low. Even if you stop partway through, this can be a good way to start, so that you get a sense of the problem.

12, 13, 14, 15, 21, 23, 24, 25, 31, 32, 34, 35, 41, 42, 43, 45, 51, 52, 53, 54 = 5 groups of 4 = 20.

4. 36: There are 3! ways in which the 3 females can swim. There are 3! ways in which the 3 males can swim. Therefore, there are 3! × 3! ways in which the entire pod can swim:

$$3! \times 3! = 6 \times 6 = 36.$$

This is a multiple arrangements problem, in which we have 2 separate pools (females and males).

5. 35: Model this problem with anagrams for the "word" YYYNNNN, in which three people are in the delegation and 4 are not:

$$\frac{7!}{3!4!} = \frac{7 \times 6 \times 5}{3 \times 2 \times 1} = 35$$ Note that you must divide by both 3! and 4! in this problem.

Alternatively, you can use the combination formula, because this problem requires the number of possible combinations of 3 delegates taken from a total of 7. (Note that order does not matter.) Therefore, the

number of possible combinations is $\dfrac{7!}{3! \times 4!} = 35$.

A	B	C	D	E	F	G
Y	Y	Y	N	N	N	N

6. 20: Consider the toppings first. Model the toppings with the "word" YYYYN, in which four of the toppings are on the pizza and one is not. The number of anagrams for this "word" is:

$$\frac{5!}{4!} = 5$$

A	B	C	D	E
Y	Y	Y	Y	N

If each of these pizzas can also be offered in 2 choices of crust, there are 5 × 2 = 10 pizzas. The same logic applies for extra-cheese and regular: 10 × 2 = 20.

Alternatively, use the combinations formula to count the combinations of toppings: $\dfrac{5!}{4! \times 1!} = 5$. Or use an intuitive approach: choosing four toppings out of five is equivalent to choosing the ONE topping that will not be on the pizza. There are clearly 5 ways to do that.

7. A: We can use the Slot Method to solve this problem. The first slot can be filled by any one of the digits from 1 through 9, since 0 is disallowed. The second digit has no restriction involving zero; however, the digit that was used in the first slot may not be reused. Thus the second slot also has nine possibilities. The third and fourth slots may not use previously used digits, so they may be filled with 8 and 7 different digits, respectively. The total number of possible postal codes is therefore

$$9 \cdot 9 \cdot 8 \cdot 7 = 4{,}536$$

the new standard

Country X has a four-digit postal code assigned to each town, such that the first digit is non-zero, and none of the digits is repeated.

Column A	Column B
The number of possible postal codes in Country X = **4,536**	4,500

8. **A:** The Anagram Grid is a good method for solving this problem. We can use the numbers 1 through 8 to uniquely designate each athlete. In the second row, G, S and B designate the three medals, while the athletes who get no medal can each be associated with an N:

Athlete	1	2	3	4	5	6	7	8
Medal	G	S	B	N	N	N	N	N

The number of ways the medals can be awarded is the number of ways the "word" GSBNNNNN can be

anagrammed. Because 5 of the letters are repeated, the answer is given by $\dfrac{8!}{5!} = \dfrac{8 \times 7 \times 6 \times 5 \times 4 \times 3 \times 2 \times 1}{5 \times 4 \times 3 \times 2 \times 1}$

$= 8 \times 7 \times 6.$

Compare this number to $8 \times 3!$.

$8 \times 3! = 8 \times 3 \times 2 \times 1 = 8 \times 6.$

Rewrite the columns:

Column A	Column B
The number of ways the medals can be awarded = **8 × 7 × 6**	$8 \times 3! = \mathbf{8 \times 6}$

9. **B:** This exercise can be regarded as two successive "pick a group" problems. First, Lothar picks 2 out of 6 Utopian stamps, and then 2 out of 4 Cornucopian stamps. Each selection may be computed according to

the general formula $\dfrac{\text{Pool!}}{(\text{In! Out!})}$. The two numbers thus obtained must then be multiplied to give the final

result:

$$\text{Total number of ways} = \left(\frac{6!}{2!\,4!}\right) \times \left(\frac{4!}{2!\,2!}\right) = \left(\frac{6 \times 5}{2 \times 1}\right) \times \left(\frac{4 \times 3}{2 \times 1}\right) = 15 \times 6 = 90$$

Column A

The number of ways Lothar can
give four stamps (two of each type)
to Peggy Sue = **90**

100

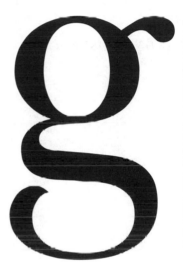

Chapter 6
of
WORD TRANSLATIONS

PROBABILITY

In This Chapter . . .

- "1" is the Greatest Probability
- More Than One Event: "AND" vs. "OR"
- The 1 − x Probability Trick
- The Domino Effect

PROBABILITY

Probability is a quantity that expresses the chance, or likelihood, of an event. In other words, it measures how often an event will occur in a long series of repeated trials.

For events with countable outcomes, probability is defined as the following fraction:

$$\text{Probability} = \frac{\text{Number of } \textit{desired} \text{ or } \textit{successful} \text{ outcomes}}{\text{Total number of } \textit{possible} \text{ outcomes}}$$

As a simple illustration, rolling a die (singular for dice) has **six** possible outcomes: 1, 2, 3, 4, 5, and 6. The probability of rolling a "5" is 1/6, because the "5" corresponds to only **one** of those outcomes. The probability of rolling a prime number, though, is 3/6 = 1/2, because in that case, three of the outcomes (2, 3, and 5) are considered successes.

For the probability fraction to be meaningful, all the outcomes must be **equally likely**. One might say, for instance, that the lottery has only two "outcomes"—win or lose—but that does not mean the probability of winning the lottery is 1/2. If you want to calculate the correct probability of winning the lottery, you must find out how many *equally likely outcomes* are possible. In other words, you have to count up all the specific combinations of differently numbered balls.

In some problems, you will have to think carefully about how to break a situation down into equally likely outcomes. Consider the following problem:

> If a fair coin is tossed three times, what is the probability that it will turn up heads exactly twice?

You may be tempted to say that there are four possibilities—no heads, 1 head, 2 heads, and 3 heads—and that the probability of 2 heads is thus ¼. You would be wrong, though, because those four outcomes are not equally likely. You are much more likely to get 1 or 2 heads than to get all heads or all tails. Instead, you have to formulate equally likely outcomes in terms of the outcome of each flip:

$$\text{HHH} \quad \text{HHT} \quad \text{HTH} \quad \text{THH} \quad \text{HTT} \quad \text{THT} \quad \text{TTH} \quad \text{TTT}$$

If you have trouble formulating this list from scratch, you can use a **counting tree**, which breaks down possible outcomes step by step, with only one decision at each branch of the tree.

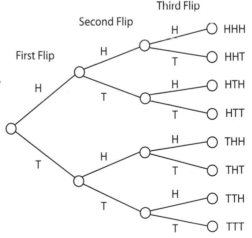

These eight outcomes are equally likely, because the coin is equally likely to come up heads or tails at each flip. Three outcomes on this list (HHT, HTH, THH) have heads exactly twice, so the probability of exactly two heads is 3/8.

This result can also be written thus:

P(exactly 2 heads) = 3/8

"1" is the Greatest Probability

The greatest probability—the certainty that an event will occur—is 1. Thus, a probability of 1 means that the event must occur. For example:

The probability that you roll a fair die once, and it lands on a number less than seven, is certain, or 1.

$$\frac{\text{Number of } \textit{successful} \text{ outcomes}}{\text{Total number of possible outcomes}} = \frac{6}{6} = \textbf{1}$$

As a percent, this certainty is expressed as 100%.

The converse is also true. The lowest probability—the impossibility that an event will occur—is 0. Thus, a probability of 0 means that an event will NOT occur. For example, the probability that you roll a fair die once and it lands on the number 9 is impossible, or 0.

$$\frac{\text{Number of } \textit{successful} \text{ outcomes}}{\text{Total number of possible outcomes}} = \frac{0}{6} = \textbf{0}$$

As a percent, this impossibility is expressed as 0%. Thus, probabilities can be percents between 0% and 100%, inclusive, or fractions between 0 and 1, inclusive.

More than One Event: "AND" vs. "OR"

Probability problems that deal with multiple events usually involve two operations: multiplication and addition. The key to understanding probability is to understand when you must multiply and when you must add.

1) Assume that X and Y are independent events. **To determine the probability that event X AND event Y will both occur, MULTIPLY the two probabilities together.**

> What is the probability that a fair coin flipped twice will land on heads both times?

This is an "AND" problem, because it is asking for the probability that the coin will land on heads on the first flip AND on the second flip. The probability that the coin will land on heads on the first flip is 1/2. The probability that the coin will land on heads on the second flip is 1/2.

Therefore, the probability that the coin will land on heads on both flips is $\frac{1}{2} \times \frac{1}{2} = \frac{1}{4}$.

Note that the probability of having BOTH flips come up heads (1/4) is less than the probability of just one flip come up heads (1/2). This should make intuitive sense. If you define success in a more constrained way (e.g., "to win, BOTH this AND that have to happen"), then the probability of success will be lower. The operation of multiplication should also make sense. Typical probabilities are fractions between 0 and 1. When you multiply together two such fractions, you get a *smaller* result, which means a lower probability.

2) Assume that X and Y are mutually exclusive events (meaning that the two events cannot both occur). **To determine the probability that event X OR event Y will occur, ADD the two probabilities together.**

What is the probability that a fair die rolled once will land on either 4 or 5?

This is an "OR" problem, because it is asking for the probability that the die will land on either 4 **or** 5. The probability that the die will land on 4 is 1/6. The probability that the die will land on 5 is 1/6. The two outcomes are mutually exclusive: the die cannot land on BOTH 4 and 5 at the same time.

Therefore, the probability that the die will land on either 4 or 5 is $\dfrac{1}{6} + \dfrac{1}{6} = \dfrac{2}{6} = \dfrac{1}{3}$.

Note that the probability of having the die come up either 4 or 5 (1/3) is greater than the probability of a 4 by itself (1/6) or of a 5 by itself (1/6). This should make intuitive sense. If you define success in a less constrained way (e.g., "I can win EITHER this way OR that way"), then the probability of success will be higher. The operation of addition should also make sense. Typical probabilities are fractions between 0 and 1. When you add together two such fractions, you get a *larger* result, which means a higher probability.

Check Your Skills

1. If a die is rolled twice, what is the probability that it will land on an even number both times?
2. Eight runners in a race are equally likely to win the race. What is the probability that the race will be won by the runner in lane 1 or the runner in lane 8?

Answers can be found on page 101.

The $1 - x$ Probability Trick

As shown on the previous page, you can solve "OR" problems (explicit or disguised) by combining the probabilities of individual events. If there are many individual events, though, such calculation may be tedious and time-consuming. The good news is that you may not have to perform these calculations. In certain types of "OR" problems, the probability of the desired event NOT happening may be much easier to calculate.

For example, in the previous section, we could have calculated the probability of getting at least one head on two flips by considering how we would NOT get at least one head. However, it was not too much work to compute the probability directly, using the slightly more complicated "OR" formula.

But let us say that a salesperson makes five sales calls, and you want to find the likelihood that he or she makes *at least one* sale. If you try to calculate this probability directly, you will have to confront five separate possibilities that constitute "success": exactly 1 sale, exactly 2 sales, exactly 3 sales, exactly 4 sales, or exactly 5 sales. You would have no choice but to calculate each of those probabilities separately and then add them together. This will be far too much work, especially under timed conditions.

However, consider the probability of *failure*—that is, the salesperson *does not* make at least one sale. Now you have only one possibility to consider: zero sales. You can now calculate the probability in which you are interested, because for *any* event, the following relationship is true:

Probability of SUCCESS + **Probability of FAILURE** = 1
(the event happens)   (it does not happen)

*If on a GRE problem, "success" contains **multiple possibilities**—especially if the wording contains phrases such as **"at least"** and **"at most"**—then consider finding the probability that success **does not happen**. If you can find this "failure" probability more easily (call it x), then the probability you really want to find will be **1 − x**.*

For example:

> What is the probability that, on three rolls of a single fair die, AT LEAST ONE of the rolls will be a six?

We could list all the possible outcomes of three rolls of a die (1–1–1, 1–1–2, 1–1–3, etc.), and then determine how many of them have at least one six, but this would be very time-consuming. Instead, it is easier to think of this problem in reverse before solving.

> Failure: What is the probability that NONE of the rolls will yield a 6?

On each roll, there is a $\dfrac{5}{6}$ probability that the die will not yield a 6.

Thus, the probability that on all 3 rolls the die will not yield a 6 is $\dfrac{5}{6} \times \dfrac{5}{6} \times \dfrac{5}{6} = \dfrac{125}{216}$.

Now, we originally defined success as rolling at least one six. Since we have found the probability of failure, we answer the original question by subtracting this probability from 1:

$$1 - \frac{125}{216} = \frac{91}{216}$$ is the probability that at least one six will be rolled.

Check Your Skills

3. If a die is rolled twice, what is the probability that it will land on an even number at least once?

Answers can be found on page 101.

The Domino Effect

Sometimes the outcome of the first event will affect the probability of a subsequent event. For example:

> In a box with 10 blocks, 3 of which are red, what is the probability of picking out a red block on each of your first two tries? Assume that you do NOT replace the first block after you have picked it.

Since this is an "AND" problem, we must find the probability of both events and multiply them together. Consider how easy it is to make the following mistake:

You compute the probability of picking a red block on your first pick as $\dfrac{3}{10}$.

You compute the probability of picking a red block on your second pick as $\dfrac{3}{10}$.

So you compute the probability of picking a red block on both picks as $\dfrac{3}{10} \times \dfrac{3}{10} = \dfrac{9}{100}$.

This solution is WRONG, because it does not take into account that the first event affects the second event. If a red block is chosen on the first pick, then the number of blocks now in the box has decreased from **10 to 9**. Additionally, the number of red blocks now in the box has decreased from **3 to 2**. Therefore,

the probability of choosing a red block on the second pick is different from the probability of choosing a red block on the first pick.

The CORRECT solution to this problem is as follows:

The probability of picking a red block on your first pick is $\dfrac{3}{10}$.

The probability of picking a red block on your second pick is $\dfrac{2}{9}$.

Therefore, the probability of picking a red block on both picks is $\dfrac{3}{10} \times \dfrac{2}{9} = \dfrac{6}{90} = \dfrac{1}{15}$.

Do not forget to analyze events by considering whether one event affects subsequent events. The first roll of a die or flip of a coin has no affect on any subsequent rolls or flips. However, the first pick of an object out of a box does affect subsequent picks if you do not replace that object. This scenario is called "without replacement."

If you <u>are</u> supposed to replace the object, the problem should clearly tell you so. In this scenario (called "with replacement"), the first pick does not affect the second pick.

Check Your Skills

4. A drawer contains 7 white shirts and 3 red shirts. What is the probability of picking a white shirt, followed by a red shirt if the first shirt is not put back in?

Answers can be found on page 101.

Check Your Skills Answers

1. **1/4:** For each throw, the probability of an even number is $3/6 = 1/2$. We multiply the individual probabilities because the two outcomes are independent: $P = 1/2 \times 1/2 = 1/4$.

2. **1/4:** $P(1) = 1/8$, $P(8) = 1/8$, $P(1 \text{ or } 8) = 1/8 + 1/8 = 1/4$.

3. **3/4:** If the die does not land on an even number at least once, then it must have landed on an odd number both times. For each throw, the probability of an odd number is $3/6 = 1/2$. Multiply the individual probabilities to get the probability of two odd numbers in a row: $x = 1/2 \times 1/2 = 1/4$. Then the probability of at least one even number is $1 - x = 1 - 1/4 = 3/4$.

4. **7/30:** There are 10 shirts total. Probability of picking a white shirt first: $7/10$.

Probability of picking a red shirt next (out of 8 remaining): $3/9 = 1/3$.

Probability of picking white first, then red: $7/10 \times 3/9 = 21/90 = 7/30$.

Problem Set

Solve the following problems. Express probabilities as fractions or percentages unless otherwise instructed.

1. What is the probability that the sum of two dice will yield a 4 or 6?

2. What is the probability that the sum of two dice will yield anything but an 8?

3. What is the probability that the sum of two dice will yield a 7, and then when both are thrown again, their sum will again yield a 7?

4. What is the probability that the sum of two dice will yield a 5, and then when both are thrown again, their sum will yield a 9?

5. At a certain pizzeria, 1/6 of the pizzas sold in a week were cheese, and 1/5 of the OTHER pizzas sold were pepperoni. If Brandon bought a randomly chosen pizza from the pizzeria that week, what is the probability that he ordered a pepperoni?

6.

A fair coin is flipped 5 times.

Column A	**Column B**
The probability of getting more heads than tails	1/2

7.

A jar contains 3 red and 2 white marbles. Two marbles are picked without replacement.

Column A	**Column B**
The probability of picking two red marbles	The probability of picking one red and one white marble

8.

A die is rolled *n* times, where *n* is at least 3.

Column A	**Column B**
The probability that at least one of the throws yields a 6	1/2

1. **2/9:** There are 36 ways in which 2 dice can be thrown ($6 \times 6 = 36$). The combinations that yield sums of 4 and 6 are $1 + 3$, $2 + 2$, $3 + 1$, $1 + 5$, $2 + 4$, $3 + 3$, $4 + 2$, and $5 + 1$: 8 different combinations. Therefore, the probability is 8/36, or 2/9.

2. **31/36:** Solve this problem by calculating the probability that the sum WILL yield a sum of 8, and then subtract the result from 1. There are 5 combinations of 2 dice that yield a sum of 8: $2 + 6$, $3 + 5$, $4 + 4$, $5 + 3$, and $6 + 2$. (Note that $7 + 1$ is not a valid combination, as there is no 7 on a standard die.) Therefore, the probability that the sum will be 8 is 5/36, and the probability that the sum will NOT be 8 is $1 - 5/36$, or 31/36.

3. **1/36:** There are 36 ways in which 2 dice can be thrown ($6 \times 6 = 36$). The combinations that yield a sum of 7 are $1 + 6$, $2 + 5$, $3 + 4$, $4 + 3$, $5 + 2$, and $6 + 1$: 6 different combinations. Therefore, the probability of rolling a 7 is 6/36, or 1/6. To find the probability that this will happen twice in a row, multiply 1/6 by 1/6 to get 1/36.

4. **1/81:** First, find the individual probability of each event. The probability of rolling a 5 is 4/36, or 1/9, since there are 4 ways to roll a sum of 5 ($1 + 4$, $2 + 3$, $3 + 2$, and $4 + 1$). The probability of rolling a 9 is also 4/36, or 1/9, since there are 4 ways to roll a sum of 9 ($3 + 6$, $4 + 5$, $5 + 4$, and $6 + 3$). To find the probability that both events will happen in succession, multiply $1/9 \times 1/9$: 1/81.

5. **1/6:** If 1/6 of the pizzas were cheese, 5/6 of the pizzas were not. 1/5 of these 5/6 were pepperoni. Multiply to find the total portion: $1/5 \times 5/6 = 1/6$. If 1/6 of the pizzas were pepperoni, there is a 1/6 chance that Brandon bought a pepperoni pizza.

6. **C:** Because heads and tails are equally likely, it follows that the probability of getting more heads than tails should be exactly the same as the probability of getting more tails than heads. The only remaining option is that we might get equally many heads and tails. However, because the total number of throws is an odd number, the latter is impossible. Therefore the probability of getting more heads than tails must be exactly 1/2. (It is, of course, also possible to compute this probability directly by considering the cases of getting 5, 4 or 3 heads separately. However, this approach would be very time consuming.)

Another way of thinking about it is that, for every throw that has more heads than tails, there is a corresponding throw, in which every throw gets the opposite result, that has more tails. For instance, the sequence of throws *HHHHH* is balanced by the sequence *TTTTT*. The sequence *HHHHT* is balanced by the throw *TTTTH*.

7. **B:** First, compute the probability of picking two red marbles. This is given by

$$P(RR) = \frac{3}{5} \times \frac{2}{4} = \frac{3}{10}.$$

Next, consider the probability of picking a red marble followed by a white marble:

$$P(RW) = \frac{3}{5} \times \frac{2}{4} = \frac{3}{10}.$$

However, this is not the only way to pick one red and one white marble; we could have picked the white

one first, followed by the red one:

$$P(WR) = \frac{2}{5} \times \frac{3}{4} = \frac{3}{10}.$$

This event is mutually exclusive from picking the red one followed by the white one. Thus, the total probability of picking one red and one white marble is the sum of the probabilities of *RW* and *WR*, yielding an

answer of $2 \times \left(\frac{3}{10} \right) = \frac{6}{10} = \frac{3}{5}.$

A jar contains 3 red and 2 white marbles. Two marbles are picked without replacement.

<u>Column A</u>	<u>Column B</u>
The probability of picking two red marbles = **3/10**	The probability of picking one red and one white marble = **3/5**

8. **D:** The easiest way to compute the probability in question is through the $1 - x$ shortcut. To do so, we imagine the opposite of the event of interest, namely, that none of the *n* throws yields a 6. The probability of a single throw not yielding a 6 is 5/6, and because each throw is independent, the cumulative probability of none of the *n* throws yielding a 6 is found by multiplication:

$$P(\text{No } 6 \text{ in } n \text{ throws}) = \left(\frac{5}{6} \right)^n$$

Powers of fractions less than one get smaller as the exponent increases. Thus, we can see that this probability will become very small for large values of *n*, such that the probability of getting at least one 6 (which is 1 minus the above) will come closer and closer to 1, which means that as *n* increases, it becomes more and more certain that a 6 will be thrown. The question now is, what is the smallest that the probability of getting at least one six could be? To answer that question, we should let *n* assume its extreme value, which is 3. In that case the probability of never getting a 6 is given by

$$P(\text{No } 6 \text{ in three throws}) = \left(\frac{5}{6} \right)^3 = \frac{125}{216}$$

such that the probability of getting at least one 6 in three throws is given by

$$P(\text{At least one } 6 \text{ in three throws}) = 1 - \frac{125}{216} = \frac{91}{216}$$

This value is less than 1/2. As we saw earlier, however, as *n* grows, it becomes ever more likely that at least one throw will yield a 6, so that the probability eventually surpasses 1/2. Thus Column A can be less than or greater than 1/2.

Chapter 7
of
WORD TRANSLATIONS

MINOR PROBLEM TYPES

In This Chapter . . .

- Optimization
- Grouping

MINOR PROBLEM TYPES

The GRE occasionally contains problems that fall under one of two umbrellas:

a. *Optimization*: maximizing or minimizing a quantity by choosing optimal values of related quantities.

b. *Grouping*: putting people or items into different groups to maximize or minimize some characteristic.

You should approach all three of these problem types with the same general outlook, although it is unlikely that you will see more than one of them on the same administration of the GRE. The general approach is to focus on **extreme scenarios**.

You should mind the following three considerations when considering any grouping or optimization problem:

1. Be aware of both **explicit constraints** (restrictions actually stated in the text) and **hidden constraints** (restrictions implied by the real-world aspects of a problem). For instance, in a problem requiring the separation of 40 people into 6 groups, hidden constraints require the number of people in each group to be a positive whole number.

2. In most cases, you can maximize or minimize quantities (or optimize schedules, etc.) by **choosing the highest or lowest values** of the variables that you are allowed to select.

3. Be very careful about **rounding**. Some problems may require you to round up, others down, and still others not at all.

Optimization

In general optimization problems, you are asked to maximize or minimize some quantity, given constraints on other quantities. These quantities are all related through some equation.

Consider the following problem:

> The guests at a football banquet consumed a total of 401 pounds of food. If no individual guest consumed more than 2.5 pounds of food, what is the minimum number of guests that could have attended the banquet?

You can visualize the underlying equation in the following table:

Pounds of food per guest	×	Guests	=	Total pounds of food
At MOST 2.5 *maximize*	×	At LEAST ??? *minimize*	=	EXACTLY 401 *constant*

Notice that finding the *minimum* value of the number of guests involves using the *maximum* pounds of food per guest, because the two quantities multiply to a constant. This sort of inversion (i.e. maximizing one thing in order to minimize another) is typical.

Begin by considering the extreme case in which each guest eats as much food as possible, or 2.5 pounds apiece. The corresponding number of guests at the banquet works out to 401/2.5 = 160.4 people.

However, you obviously cannot have a fractional number of guests at the banquet. Thus the answer must be rounded. To determine whether to round up or down, consider the explicit constraint: the amount of food per guest is a *maximum* of 2.5 pounds per guest. Therefore, the *minimum* number of guests is 160.4 (if guests could be fractional), and we must *round up* to make the number of guests an integer: 161.

Note the careful reasoning required! Although the phrase "*minimum* number of guests" may tempt you to round down, you will get an incorrect answer if you do so. In general, as you solve this sort of problem, put the extreme case into the underlying equation, and solve. Then round appropriately.

Check Your Skills

1. If no one in a group of friends has more than $75, what is the smallest number of people who could be in the group if the group purchases a flat-screen TV that costs $1,100?

Answers can be found on page 111.

Grouping

In grouping problems, you make complete groups of items, drawing these items out of a larger pool. The goal is to maximize or minimize some quantity, such as the number of complete groups or the number of leftover items that do not fit into complete groups. As such, these problems are really a special case of optimization. One approach is to determine the **limiting factor** on the number of complete groups. That is, if you need different types of items for a complete group, figure out how many groups you can make with each item, ignoring the other types (as if you had unlimited quantities of those other items). Then compare your results.

> Orange Computers is breaking up its conference attendees into groups. Each group must have exactly one person from Division A, two people from Division B, and three people from Division C. There are 20 people from Division A, 30 people from Division B, and 40 people from Division C at the conference. What is the smallest number of people who will not be able to be assigned to a group?

The first step is to find out how many groups you can make with the people from each division separately, ignoring the other divisions. There are enough Division A people for 20 groups, but only enough Division B people for 15 groups (= 30 people ÷ 2 people per group). As for Division C, there are only enough people for 13 groups, since 40 people ÷ 3 people per group = 13 groups, plus one person left over. So the limiting factor is Division C: only 13 complete groups can be formed. These 13 groups will take up 13 Division A people (leaving 20 − 13 = 7 left over) and 26 Division B people (leaving 30 − 26 = 4 left over). Together with the 1 Division C person left over, 1 + 4 + 7 = 12 people will be left over in total.

For some grouping problems, you may want to think about the **most or least evenly distributed** arrangements of the items. That is, assign items to groups as evenly (or unevenly) as possible to create extreme cases.

Check Your Skills

2. A salad dressing requires oil, vinegar and water in the ratio 2 : 1 : 3. If Oliver has 1 cup of oil, 1/3 cup of vinegar and 2 cups of water, what is the maximum number of cups of dressing that he can mix?

Answers can be found on page 111.

Check Your Skills Answers

1. **15:** The group will be as small as possible when everyone contributes as much as they're able to. The most anyone can contribute is $75, so assume that everyone contributes $75.

$$1,100 \div 75 = 14 \ 2/3$$

14 people contributing $75 would only give $1,050. Therefore you need to round up. The smallest number of people that could be in the group is 15.

2. **2 cups:** Try the limits: If Oliver used 1 cup of oil, his recipe would require 1/2 cup of vinegar and $1\frac{1}{2}$ cups of water. He does not have enough vinegar. If he used 1/3 cup of vinegar, he would need 2/3 cups of oil and 1 cup of water, both of which he has. He would then have 2/3 + 1/3 + 1 = 2 cups of dressing. He cannot possibly make more dressing than this, because he does not have any more vinegar.

Problem Set

1. Velma has exactly one week to learn all 71 Japanese hiragana characters. If she can learn at most a dozen of them on any one day and will only have time to learn four of them on Friday, what is the least number of hiragana that Velma will have to learn on Saturday?

2. Huey's Hip Pizza sells two sizes of square pizzas: a small pizza that measures 10 inches on a side and costs $10, and a large pizza that measures 15 inches on a side and costs $20. If two friends go to Huey's with $30 apiece, how many more square inches of pizza can they buy if they pool their money than if they each purchase pizza alone?

3. An eccentric casino owner decides that his casino should only use chips in $5 and $7 denominations. Which of the following amounts cannot be paid out using these chips?

   $31 $29 $26 $23 $21

4. A "Collector's Coin Set" contains a one dollar coin, a fifty-cent coin, a quarter (= 25 cents), a dime (= 10 cents), a nickel (= 5 cents), and a penny (= 1 cent). The Coin Sets are sold for the combined face price of the currency. If Colin buys as many Coin Sets as he can with the $25 he has, how much change will Colin have left over?

5.

Susan is writing a novel that will be 950 pages long when finished. She can write 10 pages per day on weekdays and 20 pages per day on weekends.

Column A	Column B
The least number of consecutive days it will take Susan to finish her novel	75

6.

Jared has four pennies (one cent), one nickel (five cents) and one dime (ten cents).

Column A	Column B
The number of different cent values that Jared can achieve using one or more of his coins	20

7.

A ribbon 40 inches long is to be cut into three pieces, each of whose lengths is a different integer number of inches.

<u>**Column A**</u>

The least possible length, in inches, of the longest piece

<u>**Column B**</u>

15

1. **7**: To minimize the number of hiragana that Velma will have to learn on Saturday, consider the extreme case in which she learns *as many* hiragana *as possible* on the other days. She learns 4 on Friday, leaving $71 - 4 = 67$ for the other six days of the week. If Velma learns the maximum of 12 hiragana on the other five days (besides Saturday), then she will have $67 - 5(12) = 7$ left for Saturday.

2. **25 square inches**: First, figure the area of each pizza: the small is 100 square inches, and the large is 225 square inches. If the two friends pool their money, they can buy three large pizzas, which have a total area of 675 square inches. If they buy individually, though, then each friend will have to buy one large pizza and one small pizza, so they will only have a total of $2(100 + 225) = 650$ square inches of pizza.

3. **$23**: This problem is similar to a Scheduling Problem in which you have a number of 5-hour and 7-hour tasks, and your mission is to figure out what total amount of time would be impossible to take. Either way, you have some integer number of 5's and some integer number of 7's. Which of the answer choices cannot be the sum? One efficient way to eliminate choices is first to cross off any multiples of 7 and/or 5: this eliminates E. Now, any other possible sums must have at least one 5 and one 7 in them. So you can subtract off 5's one at a time until you reach a multiple of 7. (It is easier to subtract 5's than 7's, because our number system is base-10.) Answer choice A: $31 - 5 = 26$; $26 - 5 = 21$, a multiple of 7; this eliminates A. (In other words, $31 = 3 \times 7 + 2 \times 5$.) Answer choice B: $29 - 5 = 24$; $24 - 5 = 19$; $19 - 5 = 14$, a multiple of 7; this eliminates B. Answer choice C: $26 - 5 = 21$, a multiple of 7; this eliminates C. So the answer must be D, 23. We check by successively subtracting 5 and looking for multiples of 7: $23 - 5 = 18$, not a multiple of 7; $18 - 5 = 13$, also not a multiple of 7; $13 - 5 = 8$, not a multiple of 7; and no smaller result will be a multiple of 7 either.

4. **$0.17**: The first step is to compute the value of a complete "Collector's Coin Set": $1.00 + $0.50 + $0.25 + $0.10 + $0.05 + $0.01 = $1.91. Now, you need to divide $1.91 into $25. A natural first move is to multiply by 10: for $19.10, Colin can buy 10 complete sets. Now add $1.91 successively. Colin can buy 11 sets for $21.01, 12 sets for $22.92, and 13 sets for $24.83. There are 17 cents left over.

5. **B:** In a week consisting of five workdays and two weekend days, Susan can write:

$$5 \times 10 + 2 \times 20 = 90 \text{ pages}$$

Therefore, in ten consecutive full weeks (i.e., 70 consecutive days), she can write 900 pages of her novel, leaving another 50 pages to be written. The least number of days it would take Susan to write 50 pages is three: two weekend days and one weekday. Thus it is possible for Susan to finish her novel in 73 days. (This assumes that Susan chooses her start day appropriately, so as to take advantage of as many weekends as possible.)

6. **B:** Jared can achieve any amount from 1 cent to 19 cents: 1 to 4 cents using the pennies, 5 cents with the nickel, 6 to 9 cents using the nickel along with the pennies, 10 cents using the dime, 11 to 14 cents using the dime along with the pennies, 15 cents using the dime and the nickel, and 16 to 19 cents using the dime and nickel along with the pennies. Notice that 19 cents requires every coin Jared possesses, meaning that 19 is the largest possible value. That makes 19 possible values.

7. **C:** Minimizing the length of the longest piece is equivalent to maximizing the lengths of the remaining pieces, as long as they are shorter than the longest piece. Suppose that the longest piece were 14 inches long (a choice motivated by wanting to be less than the 15 in Column B). That would leave $40 - 14 = 26$ inches to be accounted for by the other two pieces.

Because each piece must be a different number of inches long, those pieces cannot each be 13 inches long. This, in turn, implies that one of the two remaining pieces would have to be more than 13 inches long—but then, that piece would be 14 inches long, again violating the constraint that each piece be of a different length. Thus the longest piece must be at least 15 inches long, and the shorter pieces would be 12 and 13 inches long, for a total of 40 inches.

Chapter 8
of
WORD TRANSLATIONS

DRILL SETS

In This Chapter . . .

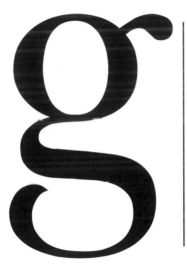

- Word Translations Drill Sets

Chapter Review: Drill Sets

DRILL SET 1:

Drill 1: Translate the following statements into equations and/or inequalities.

1. The total amount of money saved equals $2,000.
2. The number of cars is three fewer than the number of trucks.
3. There are twice as many computers as there are printers.
4. John ran twice as far as Mary.
5. There are 35 marbles in the jar, some green and some blue.

Drill 2: Translate the following statements into equations and/or inequalities.

1. Container *A* is three times as big as Container *B*.
2. One half of the students are learning French.
3. Max earned one-third of what Jerome earned.
4. The number of people on the team is three times the number of employees, minus four.
5. There are 10 more grapes than apples, and one-fourth as many apples as pears.

DRILL SET 2:

Drill 1: Translate and solve the following problems.

1. There are five more computers in the office than employees. If there are 10 employees in the office, how many computers are there?

2. If −5 is 7 more than z, what is $z/4$?

3. Each player on the team is required to purchase a uniform that costs $25. If there are 20 players on the team, what will be the total cost of the uniforms?

4. There are two trees in the front yard of a school. The trees have a combined height of 60 feet, and the taller tree is 3 times the height of the shorter tree. How high is the shorter tree?

5. A clothing store bought a container of 100 shirts for $20. If the store sold all of the shirts at $0.50 per shirt, what is the store's gross profit on the container?

Drill 2: Translate and solve the following problems.

1. A bag of 60 marbles is separated into two groups. If the first group contains 16 more marbles than the second group, how many marbles are in the larger group?

2. Two parking lots can hold a total of 115 cars. The Green lot can hold 35 fewer cars than the Red lot. How many cars can the Red lot hold?

3. At the county fair, two people are competing to see who can eat the most hot dogs. One competitor eats 7 less than the other competitor. If the competitor who eats fewer hot dogs eats 25 hot dogs, how many hot dogs did the two people eat, combined?

4. Ben and Sarah ran a combined 30 kilometers. Ben ran 8 kilometers fewer than Sarah did. How many kilometers did Ben run?

5. A class went to a donut shop, where 13 of the students ate 3 donuts each. The remaining 7 students were really hungry, and ate 8 donuts each. How many total donuts did the class eat?

Drill 3: Translate and solve the following problems.

1. Three friends sit down to eat 14 slices of pizza. If two of the friends eat the same number of slices, and the third eats two more slices than each of the other two, how many slices are eaten by the third friend?

2. A plane leaves Chicago in the morning, and makes three flights before returning. The first flight traveled twice as far as the second flight, and the second flight traveled three times as far as the third flight. If the third flight was 45 miles, how many miles was the first flight?

3. A rubber ball is thrown and bounces twice before it is caught. The first time the ball bounces it goes 5 times as high as the second time it bounces. If the second bounce goes 5 feet high, what is the combined height of the two bounces?

4. A museum tour guide can take 1 class through the museum in 30 minutes. If all classes have 30 students, how many students could go through the museum in 2 hours?

5. A band on a concert tour played 10 concerts. The first concert attracted 100 people, and the last concert attracted six times as many people. If the sixth concert attracted 1/2 as many people as the last concert, how many people were at the sixth concert?

Drill 4: Translate and solve the following problems.

1. Movie theater X charges $6 per ticket, and each movie showing costs the theatre $1,750. If 300 people bought tickets for a certain showing, and the theater averaged $2 in concessions (popcorn, etc.) per ticket-holder, what was the theater's profit for that showing?

2. Three health clubs are competing to attract new members. One company runs an ad campaign and recruits 120 new members. The second company runs a similar campaign and recruits 2/3 as many members. The third company recruits 10 more members than the second company. How many new members are recruited by the three companies combined?

3. It costs a certain bicycle factory $10,000 to operate for one month, plus $300 for each bicycle produced during the month. Each of the bicycles sells for a retail price of $700. The gross profit of the factory is measured by total income from sales minus the production costs of the bicycles. If 50 bicycles are produced and sold during the month, what is the factory's gross profit?

4. If a harbor cruise can shuttle 50 people per trip, and each trip takes 3 hours, how long will it take for 350 people to complete the tour?

5. Alfred and Nick cooked a total of 49 pies. If twice the number of pies that Alfred cooked was 14 pies more than the number of pies that Nick cooked, how many pies did Alfred cook?

ManhattanGRE Prep
the new standard

Drill 5: Translate and solve the following problems.

1. Arnaldo earns $11 for each ticket that he sells, and a bonus of $2 per ticket for each ticket he sells over 100. If Arnaldo was paid $2,400, how many tickets did he sell?

2. Alicia is producing a magazine that costs $3 per magazine to print. In addition, she has to pay $10,500 to her staff to design the issue. If Alicia sells each magazine for $10, how many magazines must she sell to break even?

3. Eleanor's football team has won 3 times as many games as Christina's football team. Christina's football team has won four fewer games than Joanna's team. If Joanna's team won 10 games last year, how many games did Eleanor's team win?

4. The distance between Town X and Town Y is twice the distance between Town X and Town Z. The distance between Town Z and Town W is 2/3 the distance between Town Z and Town X. If the distance between Town Z and Town W is 18 miles, how far is Town X from Town Y?

5. Every week, Renee is paid 40 dollars per hour for the first 40 hours she works, and 80 dollars per hour for each hour she works after the first 40 hours. If she earned $2,000 last week, how many hours did she work?

DRILL SET 3:

Drill 1: Translate and solve the following word problems involving age.

1. Norman is 12 years older than Michael. In 6 years, he will be twice as old as Michael. How old is Norman now?

2. Louise is three times as old as Mary. In 5 years, Louise will be twice as old as Mary. How old is Mary now?

3. Chris is 14 years younger than Sam. In 3 years, Sam will be 3 times as old as Chris. How old is Sam now?

4. Toshi is 7 years older than his brother Kosuke, who is twice as old as their younger sister Junko. If Junko is 8 years old, how old is Toshi?

5. Amar is 30 years younger than Lauri. In 5 years, Lauri will be three times as old as Amar. How old will Lauri be in 10 years?

Drill 2: Translate and solve the following word problems involving averages. For the purpose of these problems "average" means the arithmetic mean.

Remember that $A = \dfrac{S}{n}$, where A = average, n = the number of terms, and S = the sum of the terms.

1. 3 lawyers earn an average of $300 per hour. How much money have they earned in total after they each worked 4 hours?

2. The average of 2, 13 and *x* is 10. What is *x*?

3. Last year, Nancy earned twice the amount of money that Janet earned. Kate earned three times the amount Janet earned. If Kate earned $45,000 last year, what was the average salary of the three women?

4. John buys 5 books with an average price of $12. If John then buys another book with a price of $18, what is the average price of the six books?

5. If the average of the five numbers $x - 3$, x, $x + 3$, $x + 4$, and $x + 11$ is 45, what is the value of *x*?

Drill 3: Translate and solve the following word problems involving rates. Remember that $d = rt$, where d = distance, r = rate and t = time.

1. Bill drove to the store at a rate of 30 miles per hour. If the store is 90 miles away, how long did it take him to get there?

2. Maria normally walks at a rate of 4 miles per hour. If she walks at one half of her normal rate, how long will it take her to walk 4 miles?

3. A train traveled at a constant rate from New York to Chicago in 9 hours. If the distance between New York and Chicago is 630 miles, how fast was the train going?

4. Randy completed a 12 mile run in 4 hours. If Betty ran 3 miles per hour faster than Randy, how long did it take her to complete the same 12 mile run?

5. A truck uses 1 gallon of gasoline every 15 miles. If the truck travels 3 hours at 60 miles per hour, how many gallons of gasoline will it use?

Drill Set Answers

DRILL SET 1:

Set 1, Drill 1:

1. The total amount of money saved equals $2,000. $m = \$2,000$

2. The number of cars is three fewer than the number of trucks. $c = t - 3$

3. There are twice as many computers as there are printers. $c = 2p$

4. John ran twice as far as Mary. $j = 2m$

5. There are 35 marbles in the jar, some green and some blue. $35 = g + b$

Set 1, Drill 2:

1. Container A is three times as big as Container B. $A = 3B$

2. One half of the students are learning French. $1/2\, S = F$

3. Max earned one-third of what Jerome earned. $M = 1/3 J$

4. The number of people on the team is three times the number $t = 3e - 4$
of employees, minus four.

5. There are 10 more grapes than apples, and one-fourth as many $g = a + 10$
apples as pears. $a = 1/4\, p$

DRILL SET 2:

Set 2, Drill 1:

1. **15 computers:** There are five more computers in the office than employees. If there are 10 employees in the office, how many computers are there?

Let c = number of computers
Let e = number of employees

$c = e + 5$

If $e = 10$, then $c = (10) + 5$
$c = 15$

2. **−3:** If −5 is 7 more than z, what is z/4? $-5 = z + 7$
$z = -12$
$z/4 = -3$

3. **$500:** Each player on the team is required to purchase a uniform that costs $25. If there are 20 players on the team, what will be the total cost of the uniforms?

Let u = cost of each uniform
Let p = number of players
Let C = the total cost of the uniforms

$C = u \times p$

If $p = 20$, and $u = \$25$, then

$C = (\$25) \times (20) = \$500$

4. **15 feet:** There are two trees in the front yard of a school. The trees have a combined height of 60 feet, and the taller tree is 3 times the height of the shorter tree. How high is the shorter tree?

Let s = the height of the shorter tree
Let t = the height of the taller tree

$s + t = 60$
$3s = t$

$s + (3s) = 60$
$4s = 60$

$s = 15$

5. **$30:** A clothing store bought a container of 100 shirts for $20. If the store sold all of the shirts at $0.50 per shirt, what is the store's gross profit on the container?

Let p = profit
Let r = revenue
Let c = cost

Profit = Revenue – Cost
$p = r - c$
$r = 100 \times \$0.50$
$c = \$20$

$p = (100 \times \$0.50) - (\$20)$
$p = \$50 - \$20 = \$30$

Set 2, Drill 2:

1. **38 marbles:** A bag of 60 marbles is separated into two groups. If the first group contains 16 more marbles than the second group, how many marbles are in the larger group?

Let f = the number of marbles in the first group
Let s = the number of marbles in the second group

$f + s = 60$
$f = s + 16$
$(s + 16) + s = 60$
$2s + 16 = 60$
$2s = 44$

$s = 22$

$f = (22) + 16 = 38$

2. 75 cars: Two parking lots can hold a total of 115 cars. The Green lot can hold 35 fewer cars than the Red lot. How many cars can the Red lot hold?

Let g = the number of cars that the Green lot can hold
Let r = the number of cars that the Red lot can hold

$g + r = 115$
$g = r - 35$

$(r - 35) + r = 115$
$2r - 35 = 115$
$2r = 150$
$r = 75$

$g = r - 35 = 75 - 35 = 40$

Red lot: 75 cars
Green lot: 40 cars

3. 57 hot dogs: At the county fair, two people are competing to see who can eat the most hot dogs. One competitor eats 7 less than the other competitor. If the competitor who eats fewer hot dogs eats 25 hot dogs, how many hot dogs did the two people eat, combined?

Let f = the number of hot dogs eaten by the first competitor (assume he or she ate fewer)
Let s = the number of hot dogs eaten by the second competitor

$f = s - 7$
$f = 25$

Therefore,

$(25) = s - 7$
$s = 32$

$25 + 32 = 57$

4. 11 miles: Ben and Sarah ran a combined 30 kilometers. Ben ran 8 kilometers fewer than Sarah did. How many kilometers did Ben run?

Let B = the number of miles run by Ben
Let S = the number of miles run by Sarah

$B + S = 30$
$B = S - 8$

$B + 8 = S$

$(B + 8) + B = 30$
$2B + 8 = 30$
$2B = 22$
$B = 11$

5. 95 donuts: A class went to a donut shop, where 13 of the students ate 3 donuts each. The remaining 7 students were really hungry, and ate 8 donuts each. How many total donuts did the class eat?

13 students ate 3 donuts each: $13 \times 3 = 39$
7 students ate 8 donuts each: $7 \times (8) = 56$

Total = $39 + 56 = 95$

Set 2, Drill 3:

1. **6 slices of pizza:** Three friends sit down to eat 14 slices of pizza. If two of the friends eat the same number of slices, and the third eats two more slices than each of the other two, how many slices are eaten by the third friend?

Let P = the number of slices of pizza eaten by each of the two friends who eat the same amount.
Let T = the number of slices of pizza eaten by the third friend.

$T = P + 2$

$P + P + T = 14$
$P + P + (P + 2) = 14$
$3P + 2 = 14$
$3P = 12$
$P = 4$

$T = P + 2 = 4 + 2 = 6$

2. **270 miles:** A plane leaves Chicago in the morning, and makes three flights before returning. The first flight traveled twice as far as the second flight, and the second flight traveled three times as far as the third flight. If the third flight was 45 miles, how many miles was the first flight?

Let F = the distance of the first flight
Let S = the distance of the second flight
Let T = the distance of the third flight

$F = 2S$
$S = 3T$
$T = 45$

$S = 3 \times (45) = 135$
$F = 2 \times (135) = 270$

3. **30 feet:** A rubber ball is thrown and bounces twice before it is caught. The first time the ball bounces it goes 5 times as high as the second time it bounces. If the second bounce goes 5 feet high, what is the combined height of the two bounces?

Let a = the height of the first bounce
Let b = the height of the second bounce

$a = 5 \times b$
$b = 5$

$a = 5 \times (5) = 25$

Total height = $a + b = 25 + 5 = 30$

4. **120 students:** A museum tour guide can take 1 class through the museum in 30 minutes. If all classes have 30 students, how many students could go through the museum in 2 hours?

If each tour takes 30 minutes, a guide can complete 4 tours in 2 hours.

4 tours × 30 students = 120 students

5. **300 people:** A band on a concert tour played 10 concerts. The first concert attracted 100 people, and the last concert attracted six times as many people. If the sixth concert attracted 1/2 as many people as the last concert, how many people were at the sixth concert?

Let f = the number of people at the first concert
Let l = the number of people at the last concert
Let s = the number of people at the sixth concert

$f = 100$
$l = 6f = 6 \times (100) = 600$
$s = 1/2\ (l) = 1/2 \times (600) = 300$

Set 2, Drill 4:

1. **$650:** Movie theater X charges $6 per ticket, and each movie showing costs the theater $1,750. If 300 people bought tickets for a certain showing, and the theater averaged $2 in concessions (popcorn, etc.) per ticket-holder, what was the theater's profit for that showing?

Profit = Revenue − Cost

Revenue = 300 × 6 + 300 × 2 = 1,800 + 600 = 2,400
Cost = 1,750

Profit = 2,400 − 1,750 = 650

2. **290 new members:** Three health clubs are competing to attract new members. One company runs an ad campaign and recruits 120 new members. The second company runs a similar campaign and recruits 2/3 as many members. The third company recruits 10 more members than the second company. How many new members are recruited by the three companies combined?

Let a = the number of new members recruited by the first company
Let b = the number of new members recruited by the second company
Let c = the number of new members recruited by the third company

$a = 120$
$b = 2/3\ (a) = 2/3 \times (120) = 80$
$c = b + 10 = (80) + 10 = 90$

$a + b + c = 120 + 80 + 90 = 290$

3. **$10,000:** It costs a certain bicycle factory $10,000 to operate for one month, plus $300 for each bicycle produced during the month. Each of the bicycles sells for a retail price of $700. The gross profit of the factory is measured by total income from sales minus the production costs of the bicycles. If 50 bicycles are produced and sold during the month, what is the factory's gross profit?

Profit = Revenue − Cost
Revenue = 50 × 700 = 35,000

Cost = 10,000 + (50 × 300) = 10,000 + 15,000 = 25,000
Profit = 35,000 − 25,000 = 10,000

4. **21 hours:** If a harbor cruise can shuttle 50 people per trip, and each trip takes 3 hours, how long will it take for 350 people to complete the tour?

First, let's figure out how many trips we need. If each trip can accommodate 50 people, then we will need:

350 people / 50 = 7 trips

7 trips × 3 hours = 21 hours

5. **21 pies:** Alfred and Nick cooked a total of 49 pies. If twice the number of pies that Alfred cooked was 14 pies more than the number of pies that Nick cooked, how many pies did Alfred cook?

Let A = the number of pies that Alfred cooked.
Let N = the number of pies that Nick cooked.

$A + N = 49$
$2A = N + 14 \quad 2A - 14 = N$

$A + (2A - 14) = 49$
$3A - 14 = 49$
$3A = 63$
$A = 21$

Set 2, Drill 5:

1. **200 tickets:** Arnaldo earns $11 for each ticket that he sells, and a bonus of $2 per ticket for each ticket he sells over 100. If Arnaldo was paid $2,400, how many tickets did he sell?

Let x = the total number of tickets sold.

Therefore, $(x - 100)$ = the number of tickets sold over 100

$11x + 2(x - 100) = 2,400$
$11x + 2x - 200 = 2,400$
$13x = 2,600$
$x = 200$

2. **1,500 magazines:** Alicia is producing a magazine that costs $3 per magazine to print. In addition, she has to pay $10,500 to her staff to design the issue. If Alicia sells each magazine for $10, how many magazines must she sell to break even?

Let m = the number of magazines sold
Total cost = $3m + 10,500$
Total revenue = $10m$

Breaking even occurs when total revenue equals total cost, so:

$3m + 10,500 = 10m$
$10,500 = 7m$
$1,500 = m$

3. **18 games:** Eleanor's football team has won 3 times as many games as Christina's football team. Christina's football team has won four fewer games than Joanna's team. If Joanna's team won 10 games last year, how many games did Eleanor's team win?

Let E = the number of games Eleanor's team won
Let C = the number of games Christine's team won
Let J = the number of games Joanna's team won

$E = 3C$
$C = J - 4$
$J = 10$

$C = (10) - 4 = 6$
$E = 3(6) = 18$

4. **54 miles:** The distance between Town X and Town Y is twice the distance between Town X and Town Z. The distance between Town Z and Town W is 2/3 the distance between Town Z and Town X. If the distance between Town Z and Town W is 18 miles, how far is Town X from Town Y?

Let $[XY]$ = the distance between Town X and Town Y
Let $[XZ]$ = the distance between Town X and Town Z
Let $[ZW]$ = the distance between Town Z and Town W

Translating the information in the question, we get:
$[XY] = 2[XZ]$ from the first sentence
$[ZW] = 2/3 [XZ]$ from the second sentence
$[ZW] = 18$ from the third sentence

$18 = 2/3 [XZ]$
$54/2 = [XZ]$
$27 = [XZ]$
$[XY] = 2(27) = 54$

5. **45 hours:** Every week, Renee is paid 40 dollars per hour for the first 40 hours she works, and 80 dollars per hour for each hour she works after the first 40 hours. If she earned \$2,000 last week, how many hours did she work?

Let h = number of hours Renee worked

$40(40) + (h - 40)(80) = 2,000$
$1,600 + 80h - 3,200 = 2,000$
$80h - 1,600 = 2,000$
$80h = 3,600$
$h = 45$

<u>DRILL SET 3:</u>

Set 3, Drill 1:

1. **18 years old:** Norman is 12 years older than Michael. In 6 years, he will be twice as old as Michael. How old is Norman now?

Let N = Norman's age now	$(N + 6)$ = Norman's age in 6 years.
Let M = Michael's age now	$(M + 6)$ = Michael's age in 6 years.
$N = M + 12$	Translate the first sentence into an equation.
$N + 6 = 2 (M + 6)$	Translate the second sentence into an equation.
$N - 12 = M$	Rewrite the first equation to put it in terms of M.
$N + 6 = 2(N - 12 + 6)$	Insert $N - 12$ for M in the second equation.
$N + 6 = 2(N - 6)$	
$N + 6 = 2N - 12$	
$18 = N$	Solve for N.

2. **5 years old:** Louise is three times as old as Mary. In 5 years, Louise will be twice as old as Mary. How old is Mary now?

Let L = Louise's age now	$(L + 5)$ = Louise's age 5 years from now
Let M = Mary's age now	$(M + 5)$ = Mary's age 5 years from now
$L = 3M$	Translate the first sentence into an equation.
$(L + 5) = 2(M + 5)$	Translate the second sentence into an equation.
$(3M + 5) = 2(M + 5)$	Insert $3M$ for L in the second equation.
$3M + 5 = 2M + 10$	Make sure you distribute the 2.
$M = 5$	Solve for M

3. **18 years old:** Chris is 14 years younger than Sam. In 3 years, Sam will be 3 times as old as Chris. How old is Sam now?

Let C = Chris' age now	$(C + 3)$ = Chris' age 3 years from now
Let S = Sam's age now	$(S + 3)$ = Sam's age 3 years from now
$C = S - 14$	Translate the first sentence into an equation.
$3(C + 3) = (S + 3)$	Translate the second sentence into an equation.
$3C + 9 = S + 3$	
$3(S - 14) + 9 = S + 3$	Insert $S - 14$ for M in the second equation.
$3S - 42 + 9 = S + 3$	
$3S - 33 = S + 3$	
$2S - 33 = 3$	

$2S = 36$
$S = 18$ Solve for S.

4. 23 years old: Toshi is 7 years older than his brother Kosuke, who is twice as old as their younger sister Junko. If Junko is 8 years old, how old is Toshi?

Let T = Toshi's age
Let K = Kosuke's age
Let J = Junko's age

$J = 8$
$B = 2 \times J = 2 \times (8) = 16$
$T = B + 7 = (16) + 7 = 23$

5. 50 years old: Amar is 30 years younger than Lauri. In 5 years, Lauri will be three times as old as Amar. How old will Lauri be in 10 years?

Let A = Amar's age now $(A + 5)$ = Amar's age 5 years from now
Let L = Lauri's age now $(L + 5)$ = Lauri's age 5 years from now

We're looking for Lauri's age in 10 years: $L + 10$

$A = L - 30$ Translate the first sentence into an equation.
$L + 5 = 3 (A + 5)$ Translate the second sentence into an equation.

$L + 5 = 3(L - 30 + 5)$ Insert $L - 30$ for A in the second equation.
$L + 5 = 3(L - 25)$
$L + 5 = 3L - 75$
$80 = 2L$
$40 = L$

Remember, we're looking for Lauri's age in 10 years:

$L + 10 = 40 + 10 = 50$

Set 3, Drill 2:

1. 3 lawyers earn an average of \$300 per hour. How much money have they earned in total after they each worked 4 hours?

Each lawyer worked 4 hours, earning \$300 per hour. $4 \times \$300 = \$1,200$

There are 3 lawyers. $\$1,200 \times 3 = \$3,600$

Answer: They earned \$3,600 in total.

2. **15:** The average of 2, 13, and x is 10. What is x?

$$A = \frac{S}{n}$$

Here, $10 = A$, S is the sum of the 3 terms $(2, 13, x)$, and 3 is the number of terms.

$$\frac{2+13+x}{3} = 10$$
$$2+13+x = 30$$
$$15+x = 30$$
$$x = 15$$

3. **$30,000:** Last year, Nancy earned twice the amount of money that Janet earned. Kate earned three times the amount Janet earned. If Kate earned $45,000 last year, what was the average salary of the three women?

Let N = the amount of money Nancy earned
Let J = the amount of money Janet earned
Let K = the amount of money Kate earned
Let A = the average salary

$N = 2J$
$K = 3J$
$K = \$45,000$
$(\$45,000) = 3J$
$\$15,000 = J$
$N = 2(\$15,000)$
$N = \$30,000$

$$\frac{N+K+J}{3} = A$$

$$\frac{\$30,000 + \$15,000 + \$45,000}{3} = A$$

$$\frac{\$90,000}{3} = A$$

$$\$30,000 = A$$

4. **$13:** John buys 5 books with an average price of $12. If John then buys another book with a price of $18, what is the average price of the six books?

$$\frac{\text{Sum}}{\text{Number}} = \text{Average}$$

First, we need to know the cost of the 5 books.

Sum = (Average)(Number) = ($12)(5) = $60

Sum of the cost of all 6 books = $60 + $18 = $78
Number of total books = 6

$$\frac{\$78}{6} = \text{Average}$$

5. 42: If the average of the five numbers $x - 3$, x, $x + 3$, $x + 4$, and $x + 11$ is 45, what is the value of x?

$$\frac{(x-3)+(x)+(x+3)+(x+4)+(x+11)}{5} = 45$$

$$\frac{5x+15}{5} = 45$$

$$x + 3 = 45$$
$$x = 42$$

Set 3, Drill 3:

1. 3 hours: Bill drove to the store at a rate of 30 miles per hour. If the store is 90 miles away, how long did it take him to get there?

Let r = rate
Let t = time
Let d = distance

$r \times t = d$
$(30 \text{ mi/hr}) \times t = 90$ miles
$t = 90/30 = 3$ hours

2. 2 hours: Maria normally walks at a rate of 4 miles per hour. If she walks at one half of her normal rate, how long will it take her to walk 4 miles?

Let r = rate
Let t = time
Let d = distance
$r = 4$ miles/hr
$1/2 \times r = 2$ miles/hr
$d = 4$ miles

$r \times t = d$
2 miles/hr $\times t = 4$ miles
$2t = 4$
$t = 2$ hours

3. 70 miles per hour: A train traveled at a constant rate from New York to Chicago in 9 hours. If the distance between New York and Chicago is 630 miles, how fast was the train going?

$d = rt$
630 miles = r(9 hours)
70 miles per hour = r

4. **2 hours:** Randy completed a 12 mile run in 4 hours. If Betty ran 3 miles per hour faster than Randy, how long did it take her to complete the same 12 mile run?

r = rate at which Randy ran
$r + 3$ = the rate at which Betty ran

12 miles = r(4 hours)
r = 3 miles per hour

$12 = (r + 3)(t)$
$12 = (3 + 3)(t)$
$12 = 6t$
$2 = t$

5. **12 gallons:** A truck uses 1 gallon of gasoline every 15 miles. If the truck travels 3 hours at 60 miles per hour, how many gallons of gasoline will it use?

Let d = distance traveled

d = (60 mph)(3 hours) = 180 miles

180 miles/15 miles per gallon = 12 gallons

Appendix

of

WORD TRANSLATIONS

2011 CHANGES TO THE GRE QUANT

In This Chapter . . .

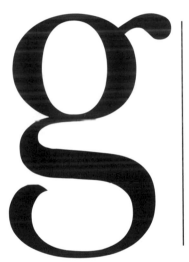

2011 Changes to the GRE Quant

In mid-2011, the Quantitative section of the GRE will undergo a number of changes. Have no fear, however—the actual body of mathematical knowledge being tested won't change, and everything in your Manhattan GRE book(s) will still be relevant and necessary to beat the test. This supplement details everything you need to know to be ready for 2011.

Currently, the GRE contains a single 45-minute quantitative section composed of multiple choice problems, Quantitative Comparisons, and Data Interpretation questions (which are really a subset of multiple choice problems).

After the 2011 changes, test takers will complete two separate 35-minute quantitative sections containing two new problem formats in addition to the current problem formats.

Additionally, a small four-function calculator with a square root will appear on-screen. Truly, many test takers will rejoice at the advent of this calculator! It is true that the GRE calculator will reduce emphasis on computation—but look out for problems in which the order of operations, or tricky wording on percents, is likely to foil those who rely on it too much.

New Problem Formats in Brief:

Multiple Choice: Select One or More Answer Choices – Questions may have from three to seven answer choices, and the test taker is asked to select a certain number of answers ("Which two of the following...") or to select all answers that meet a certain criterion ("Select all that apply").

Numeric Entry – Instead of selecting a multiple-choice answer, test takers type an answer into an entry box, or two entry boxes above and below a fraction bar.

Data Interpretation questions will also occur more often, and the above new problem types will also be used on Data Interpretation; that is, you will be presented with charts or graphs and asked a mix of Multiple Choice: Select One, Multiple Choice: Select One or More, and Numeric Entry questions.

We're about to discuss strategies for each new problem type. But overall, don't worry! The same core mathematical skills are being tested, and any time you've put into studying for the pre-2011 GRE will still be useful for the 2011 GRE. Also, as you're about to see, many of these problem types aren't as different as they might seem.

Finally, don't worry about whether these new problem types are "harder" or "easier." You're being judged against other students, all of whom are in the same boat. So if the new formats are harder, they're harder for other test takers as well. The upcoming strategies and problem sets will put you ahead of the game!

Multiple Choice: Select One or More Answer Choices

The official directions for "Select One or More Answer Choices" read as follows:

> <u>Directions:</u> Select one or more answer choices according to the specific question directions.
>
> If the question does not specify how many answer choices to select, select all that apply.
>
> The correct answer may be just one of the choices or as many as all of the choices, depending on the question.
>
> No credit is given unless you select all of the correct choices and no others.
>
> If the question specifies how many answer choices to select, select exactly that number of choices.

Note that there is no "partial credit." If three of six choices are correct and you select two of the three, no credit is given. It will also be important to read the directions carefully.

That said, many of these questions look *very* similar to those you've studied for the "old" GRE. For instance, here is a question that could have appeared on the GRE at any time:

If $ab = |a| \times |b|$, which of the following *must* be true?

I. $a = b$
II. $a > 0$ and $b > 0$
III. $ab > 0$

A.   II only
B.   III only
C.   I and III only
D.   II and III only
E.   I, II, and III

Solution: If $ab = |a| \times |b|$, then we know ab is positive, since the right side of the equation must be positive. If ab is positive, however, that doesn't necessarily mean that a and b are each positive; it simply means that they have the same sign.

I.   It is not true that a must equal b. For instance, a could be 2 and b could be 3.
II.   It is not true that a and b must each be positive. For instance, a could be -3 and b could be -4.
III. True. Since $|a| \times |b|$ must be positive, ab must be positive as well.

The answer is B (III only).

Note that, if you determined that statement I was false, you could eliminate choices C and E before considering the remaining statements. Then, if you were confident that II was also false, you could safely pick answer choice B, III only, without even trying statement III, since "None of the above" isn't an option.

the new standard

That is, because of the multiple choice answers, it is sometimes not necessary to consider each statement individually. This is the aspect of such problems that will change on the 2011 exam.

Here is the same problem, in 2011 format.

If $ab = |a| \times |b|$, which of the following *must* be true?

Indicate <u>all</u> such statements.

    A. $a = b$
    B. $a > 0$ and $b > 0$
    C. $ab > 0$

Strategy Tip: Make sure to fully "process" the statement in the question (simplify it or list the possible scenarios) before considering the answer choices. This will save you time in the long run!

Here, we would simply select choice C. The only thing that has changed is that we can't do process of elimination; we must always consider each statement individually. On the upside, the problem has become much more straightforward and compact (not every real-life problem has exactly five possible solutions; why should those on the GRE?)

Numeric Entry

The official directions for "Numeric Entry" read as follows:

> Directions: Enter your answer in the answer box(es) below the question.
>
> Equivalent forms of the correct answer, such as 2.5 and 2.50, are all correct. Fractions do not need to be reduced to lowest terms.
>
> Enter the exact answer unless the question asks you to round your answer.

Strategy Tip. Note that you are not required to reduce fractions. It may feel strange to type 9/27 instead of 1/3, but if you're not required to reduce, why take an extra step that has the possibility of introducing a mistake?

In this problem type, you are not able to "work backwards" from answer choices, and in many cases it will be difficult to make a guess. However, the principles being tested are just the same as on the old GRE.

Here is a sample question:

If $x*y = 2xy - (x - y)$, what is the value of 3*4 ?

Solution:

We are given a function involving two variables, x and y, and asked to substitute 3 for x and 4 for y:

$$x * y = 2xy - (x - y)$$
$$3 * 4 = 2(3)(4) - (3 - 4)$$
$$3 * 4 = 24 - (-1)$$
$$3 * 4 = 25$$

The answer is 25.

Thus, you would type 25 into the box.

Using the Calculator

The addition of a small, four-function calculator with a square root means that those taking the 2011 test can forget re-memorizing their times tables or square roots. However, the calculator is not a cure-all; in many problems, the difficulty is in figuring out what numbers to put into the calculator in the first place. In some cases, using a calculator will actually be less helpful than doing the problem some other way.

On the new 2011 GRE, you will be provided with a simple on-screen calculator. For this practice set, you may use any calculator, but don't use any functions other than $+$, $-$, $\times$, $\div$, and $\sqrt{}$.

If x is the remainder when (11)(7) is divided by 4 and y is the remainder when (14)(6) is divided by 13, what is the value of $x + y$?

Solution: This problem is designed so that the calculator won't tell the whole story. Certainly the calculator will tell us that $11 \times 7 = 77$. When you divide 77 by 4, however, the calculator yields an answer of 19.25. The remainder is *not* 0.25 (a remainder is always a whole number).

You might just go back to your pencil and paper, and find the largest multiple of 4 that is less than 77. Since 4 DOES go into 76, we can conclude that 4 would leave a remainder of 1 when dividing into 77. (Notice that we don't even need to know how many times 4 goes into 76, just that it goes in. One way to mentally "jump" to 76 is to say, *4 goes into 40, so it goes into 80… that's a bit too big, so take away 4 to get 76*).

However, it is also possible to use the calculator to find a remainder. Divide 77 by 4 to get 19.25. Thus, 4 goes into 77 nineteen times, with a remainder left over. Now use your calculator to multiply 19 (JUST 19, not 19.25) by 4. You will get 76. The remainder is $77 - 76 = 1$. Therefore, $x = 1$.

Use the same technique to find y. Multiply 14×6 to get 84. Divide 84 by 13 to get 6.46… Ignore everything after the decimal, and just multiply 6 by 13 to get 78. The remainder is therefore $84 - 78 = 6$. Therefore, $y = 6$.

Since we are looking for $x + y$ and $1 + 6 = 7$, the answer is 7.

2011 Format Word Translations Questions

On the new 2011 GRE, you will be provided with a simple on-screen calculator. For this practice set, you may use any calculator, but don't use any functions other than +, −, ×, ÷, and √.

1. A room contains 6 boys and 15 girls. Which TWO of the following would cause the ratio of boys to girls to become at least 2 to 3?

    A. 10 boys join and 10 girls join
    B. 4 boys join and no girls leave
    C. 20 boys join and 30 girls join
    D. 1 boy joins and 5 girls leave

2. Together, fries and a drink cost $7. 2 fries, 2 drinks, and 4 cookies cost $20 total. What is the ratio of the price of one cookie to the price of fries and a drink together?

3. Josie lives at least 2 miles from school. Some days she walks at a rate of 3 miles per hour, and some days she rides her bike at a rate of 7 miles per hour. Which of the following could be the amount of time Josie spends getting to school?

    Indicate all such statements.

    A. 10 minutes
    B. 12 minutes
    C. 15 minutes
    D. 20 minutes
    E. 48 minutes
    F. 144 minutes

4. Two people were hired to distribute 1,000 flyers total. One person distributed 120 flyers at a rate of 40 flyers per hour, and then both people worked together distributing flyers at a combined rate of 110 flyers per hour until all the flyers were gone. If the two people split the $190 payment in proportion to the number of hours worked, how much did the person who worked longer receive? Disregard the dollar sign in entering your answer.

1. This is a ratios problem. We need the ratio of boys to girls to become at least 2/3, which is 0.6666... in your calculator.

A. If 10 boys join and 10 girls join, we have 16 boys to 25 girls. Put 16/25 in your calculator to get 0.64. Do NOT pick A.

B. If 4 boys join and no girls leave, we have 10 boys and 15 girls. This is exactly 2/3. Since the problem says "at least," this qualifies. B is correct.

C. If 20 boys and 30 girls join, we have 26 boys and 45 girls. Put 26/45 in your calculator to get 0.57.... Do NOT pick C.

D. If 1 boy joins and 5 girls leave, we have 7 boys and 10 girls. This is more than 2/3. You can also put 7/10 in your calculator to get 0.7. D is correct.

The answer is B and D.

2. This is an algebraic translations problem. Fries and a drink cost $7, and 2 fries, 2 drinks, and 4 cookies cost $20. Let f = cost of fries, d = cost of a drink and c = cost of a cookie. Thus:

$$f + d = 7$$

$$2f + 2d + 4c = 20$$

We can simplify the second equation by diving through by 2.

$$f + d + 2c = 10$$

Although we have three variables and only two equations, we will still be able to solve for c, because the *combination* $(f + d)$ is equal to 7. So substitute 7 in place of $(f + d)$ in the second equation:

$$(7) + 2c = 10$$

$$2c = 3$$

$$c = 1.5$$

We do not have enough information to solve for f and d individually, but we don't need to. The question asks for the ratio of c to $f + d$.

$$\frac{1.5}{7}$$

To normalize this ratio, just double the top and the bottom:

$$\frac{3}{14}$$

The answer is $\dfrac{3}{14}$.

3. This is a Rates problem that uses ranges. Josie lives "at least two miles" from school. This range is bounded in only one direction—that is, she may live a million miles from school, in which case it would take her a really, really long time to walk there. Essentially, no answer could be too large. (Since at least one answer must be correct, we can already conclude that the largest answer, F, is correct).

So we're really concerned about the lower end of the range. How fast could she possibly get there?

The distance is "greater than 2" and Josie's fastest rate is 7 mph. From Rate × Time = Distance:

$$7t = \text{"greater than 2"}$$

$$t = \frac{\text{"greater than 2"}}{7}$$

The bigger the top of the fraction gets, the bigger t will get. If the numerator were actually 2, t would equal 2/7, so we can conclude that t must actually be greater than 2/7 (since the distance is not actually allowed to be equal to 2).

Thus, any time longer than 2/7 of an hour is valid.

Put 2/7 in the calculator to get 0.2857....

Multiply by 60 to convert to minutes. You get 17.14... minutes. This is the minimum time it takes Josie to get to school.

The correct answer is D, E, and F.

4. This is a work problem. Remember, Rate × Time = Work. One person distributes 120 flyers at 40 flyers per hour. Thus 40 × Time = 120, and Time = 3 hours. Also, there are now 880 (1,000 − 120) flyers left to distribute.

Then, the two people work together distributing flyers at 110 flyers/hour until the remaining 880 flyers are gone. Thus, 110 × Time = 880. Time = 8 hours. That is, EACH PERSON worked 8 hours.

Thus, the first person worked 3 hours and then another 8 hours. The second person worked only 8 hours.

Overall, 19 hours were worked. The $190 payment works out to $10 per hour.

The first person, who worked 11 hours, would receive $110.

The answer is 110.

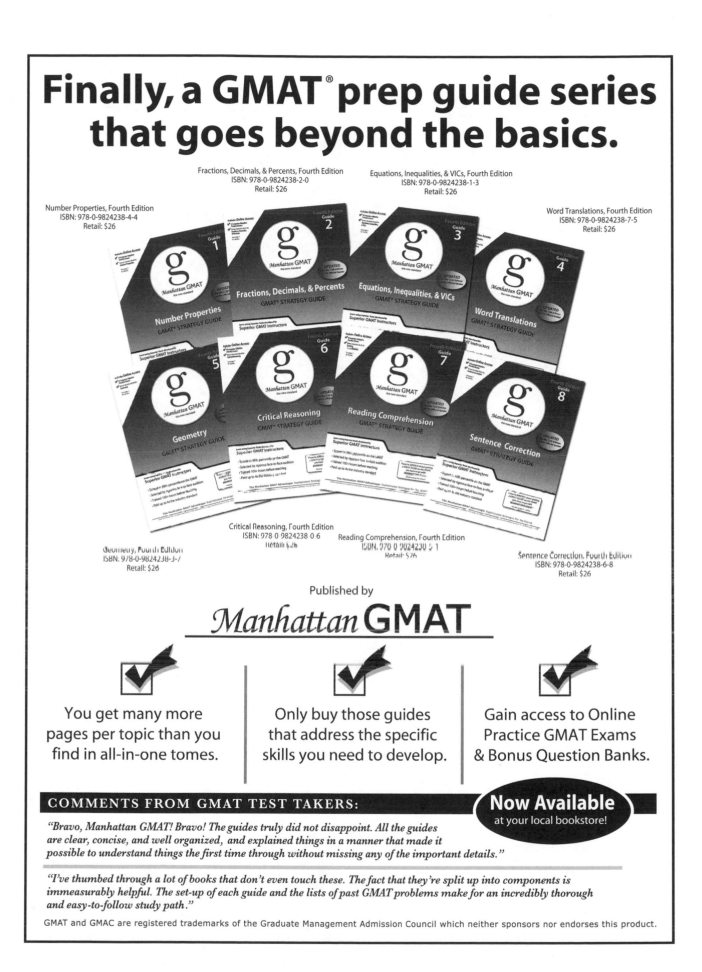